The
Mandala
Bible

The
Mandala
Bible

The definitive guide to using sacred shapes

Madonna Gauding

A FIREFLY BOOK

Published by Firefly Books Ltd. 2011

Copyright © Octopus Publishing Group Ltd 2011

Text copyright © Madonna Gauding 2011

First printing

Publisher Cataloging-in-Publication Data (U.S.)

Gauding, Madonna.

The Mandala bible : the definitive guide to using sacred shapes / Madonna Gauding.

[400] p. : ill., col. photos. ; cm.

Includes index.

Summary: This comprehensive book introduces the reader to the many different forms a Mandala can take, from ancient Hindu Mandalas to the intricate patterns of Native American sand paintings and Celtic knot work. It also provides practical information on how to use a Mandala to promote spiritual health and wellbeing.

ISBN-13: 978-1-55407-890-5 (pbk.)

1. Mandala. I. Title.

291.37 dc22   BL604.M36G373   2011

Library and Archives Canada Cataloguing in Publication

A CIP record of this book is available from Library and Archives Canada

Published in the United States by
Firefly Books (U.S.) Inc.
P.O. Box 1338, Ellicott Station
Buffalo, New York 14205

Published in Canada by
Firefly Books Ltd.
66 Leek Crescent
Richmond Hill, Ontario L4B 1H1

Printed in China

Contents

Introduction
to mandalas

What is a 'mandala'?

The word 'mandala' comes from the classical Sanskrit language. It is made up of the words *mand*, meaning 'to mark off', and *la*, meaning 'circle' or 'sacred centre'. Sometimes 'mandala' is translated as 'essence container', a phrase that hints at its psychological and mystical meanings.

Within the Hindu and Buddhist traditions the mandala is a sacred symbol of the spiritual journey, and a two-dimensional pictorial representation of a multi-dimensional divine universe. The symbols and figures in these elaborate painted mandalas merely suggest what they represent – experience of the absolute nature of reality in all its splendour and bliss, and the realization of enlightenment. The Hindu and Buddhist paths are similar, but different: the Hindu path is about realization of the self as one with the divine, whereas the Buddhist path emphasizes Buddha-nature, or the potential for enlightenment. But for both traditions the elaborate pictorial representations of the mandala symbolize the unseen aspects of reality and serve as an aid to spiritual development.

Mandalas down the ages

The use of the mandala, or circle form, is not limited to Hindu and Buddhist traditions. Since prehistoric times humans have instinctively used the circle to symbolize all aspects of human and planetary existence, from the secular to the spiritual, from the profane to the profound. For example, the mandala appears in prehistoric and indigenous art: in the spirals incised on stones at Neolithic sites; in pictograph circles carved on rocks in the American south-west; and in the symbols drawn by South Asian women at the entrance of houses to ward off negative energy.

Early Christians made extensive use of the mandala as a teaching device, first in the form of paintings on church walls, and later as magnificent stained-glass rose windows. In modern times the psychologist Carl Jung

(1875–1961) used the mandala as a tool for psychological wholeness. And today the mandala appears in the dome architecture of Buckminster Fuller and in the earth sculptures of British artist Andy Goldsworthy.

A Jain diagram of Jambudvipa (the Universe) that depicts the mythological Mount Meru, axis of the world.

Why work with mandalas?

The stresses of modern life may leave you feeling disconnected from your authentic self and separated from your deepest needs and desires. Working with mandalas will help you reconnect with your body, mind and spirit so that you feel whole and integrated, rather than stressed and pulled apart.

Mandalas will also help you reconnect to nature and the Earth. But perhaps most importantly, mandalas are a communication tool for connecting with God, your higher self, your inner self or the 'source' – in other words, that which is greater than yourself.

Many people use mandalas for meditation and contemplation; others use them for therapy and healing. Some people colour in mandalas in order to relax and centre themselves. Carl Jung used mandalas extensively with his patients, who would create them as a means to connect with their subconscious, enabling them to work through their issues. For a period of time Jung created a mandala every day – an activity that he credits with his personal transformation and healing. Many psychologists, therapists and cancer centres today use mandalas (and colouring them) as a form of therapy.

Union of body, mind and soul

In our modern culture we are often profoundly disconnected from our bodies. The act of colouring and drawing mandalas while working with personal, psychological or spiritual issues brings your body and soul into alignment with your deepest needs and highest intentions. The rhythmic movements of colouring or drawing engage the body in the same way that prayer beads enhance the recitation of mantras in the Buddhist tradition, or the recitation of prayers in the Catholic and Muslim traditions. The prayer beads are not just for counting, but also for bringing body and soul together in the activity of prayer. Colouring, drawing or painting the archetypal form of the mandala, while being engaged in meditation or contemplation, brings body, mind and soul together in one unified effort.

The mandala is not just any form; rather, it represents the sacred, the primordial and the infinite. It resonates with, and reflects, the many forms of nature, the Earth and the cosmos. The following pages will help you better understand the sources of the mandala's power and meaning.

Colouring mandalas is a powerful method for overcoming stress and connecting with your deeper self.

The circle as symbol of the universe

The mandala represents the circle, the primal form of the universe itself from which all other forms are derived. The sun and moon are circles, as are the billions of stars in the night sky.

Photographs from the Hubble space telescope reveal in awesome detail the spiral galaxies and circular movement of the planets. We know the Earth itself is a huge ball hurtling through space, circling around the fiery orb of our life-giving sun. But, oddly, even in our technological scientific age, we still experience the sun 'moving' across the sky in a great arc. Like all humanity before us, we imagine that it is the fiery yellow orb that moves – 'rising' in the east and 'setting' in the west – rather than the Earth on which we reside.

In our dynamic, ever-changing world, atoms and cells endlessly combine to create the myriad forms of existence. A flower, a snowflake or a cross-section of a tree – each reveals growth moving outward from a central point. The Hindus called this point a *bindu*, or sacred point, the source from which everything that exists

Spiral galaxies in outer space are among nature's most awe-inspiring and beautiful forms.

emanates. In the Hindu mandala known as the Shri Yantra (see pages 166–73) the circle represents the *yoni* or vulva and the *bindu* in its centre represents the seed or sperm. The *yoni*, the female organ, gives birth to the world and to time, and the *lingam*, or male organ, produces the seed of being.

The opposing forces of Yin and Yang

For the ancient Taoists of China an empty circle symbolized Wu Chi or Tao, a pregnant void from which the universe emerged. Wu Chi then gave birth to a primordial organic unity, from which emerged two opposite forces, Yin and Yang (see above right). These dynamic forces ceaselessly interpenetrate each other, giving birth to 'myriad beings'.

Form and formlessness

Modern physics speculates that the universe came into existence from the 'Big Bang', an explosion from a single primeval atom, which may have simultaneously embodied both form and formlessness. For the great Japanese Zen abbot Sengai (1750–1837), the circle represented

A circular yin and yang symbol on a temple door in South Korea reminds adherents of sacred truths.

infinity, the origin of all beings – but infinity itself was formless. Mathematicians also tell us that a circle has a centre, but the point at the centre of the circle is dimensionless.

The mandala symbolizes the ineffable sacredness at the centre of everyday reality. That sacredness – the centre of the circle – is formless and dimensionless, boundless and eternal, with no beginning and no end. As reflected in the Buddhist Heart Sutra, 'All things are empty: Nothing is born, nothing dies.'

The atom as mandala

The atom is the building block of the universe. It is a basic unit
of matter that consists of a dense central nucleus surrounded
by a cloud of negatively charged electrons.

The nucleus contains a mix of
positively charged protons and
electrically neutral neutrons. The
electrons of an atom are bound to
the nucleus by electromagnetic force.
Atoms are minuscule objects with
tiny masses. They are so small they
can only be observed using special
instruments, such as the scanning
tunnelling microscope. The nucleus,
the space around the nucleus and the
shell of the atom are the blueprint
of the mandala form. This atomic
mandala form repeats itself endlessly
– in the universe, and in the natural
world of Planet Earth.

The word 'atom' comes from
the Greek *átomos*, which means
'uncuttable' or 'indivisible' –
something that cannot be divided
further. However, during the late 19th
and early 20th centuries physicists
discovered subatomic components
and structure inside the atom, thereby

demonstrating that the atom was
divisible. The principles of quantum
mechanics led to a rethinking of the
structure of the atom.

The paradox of wave–particle duality

A central concept of quantum
mechanics is wave–particle duality,
which arose to address the inability of
classical concepts to fully describe the
behaviour of quantum-scale objects.
Some say that this paradox – that
something can be both a particle and
a wave – is a fundamental property of
the universe, while others say that it
arises because of various limitations
of the observer. Whatever it is, this
phenomenon has been verified not
only for elementary particles, but also
for compound particles like atoms
and molecules. In fact, wave–particle
duality applies to all objects, even
those we can see. But because of their

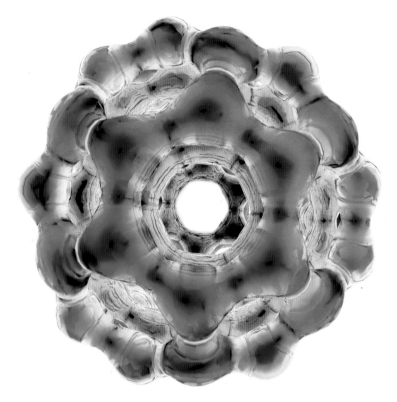

small wavelengths, we cannot see the wave properties of everyday objects.

The mandala reflects quantum theory because the mandala is a dynamic symbol of both the form and the energy of the universe. The mandala principle simultaneously

A Buckminsterfullerene molecule of carbon has a mandala-like structure resembling Fuller's geodesic domes.

embodies particle and wave, matter and energy, and the material and the spiritual aspects of life.

The circle in nature

If you live in an urban area, you may spend most of your time either in your home or your place of work. In fact, you may spend 90 per cent of your time indoors or in a car, bus, train or plane.

If you are lucky, you may find time to be outdoors on the weekend, perhaps working in your yard or garden, or taking the dog for a longer walk. But, with your mind filled with the pressures of work and other responsibilities, nature may be the last thing on your mind. Yet being cut off from nature is harming all of us and causing untold harm to the Earth and to future generations.

Reconnecting with nature
Working with the mandala, which is itself a profound symbol of nature, is one of the best ways to find your way back to the natural world. The experience of colouring and creating mandalas will help you comprehend both yourself and nature differently.

Working with the mandala may inspire you to feel more at one with the natural world.

The mandala becomes a bridge to understanding the true nature of yourself and the world around you. Rather than something to be observed from afar, or something to use, or even something to fear, the natural world will begin to feel more like home. The trees, plants and animals, and even the stars above, will start to seem like the close relatives they are, because you and the natural world are one.

As you work physically, mentally and emotionally with a mandala, which represents the primordial circle of existence, you will find yourself more in alignment with the natural rhythms of the Earth. You will feel less static, separate and alienated, and you will begin to experience yourself as a dynamic and interdependent being residing in a vibrant, pulsating and amazingly creative universe. Even if the details of your life remain the same – same house, same job, same schedule – by working with the mandala you will understand, more profoundly than ever, that you and nature are one.

This knowledge of being one with the natural world comes through the body, through the act of colouring, meditating on and relating to the mandala. By reconnecting with your body and the sensuousness of the physical world, you will become more eager to reconnect with the natural world.

The cell and the mandala

The word 'cell' comes from the Latin *cellula*, meaning a 'small room'.
Cells in nature function much like the enclosed form of the mandala.
They are containers of life energy and hereditary information.

Its similarity to the cell – the
essential structure of all living things
– is one reason the mandala form
speaks to us on such a primal level.
All biological life is composed of
mandala-like cells that divide and
multiply, to create the myriad forms
that make up the natural world.

The origin of cells has to do with
the origin of life. There are several
theories about the origin of these small
molecules that led to life on an early
Earth. One is that they came from
meteorites; another is that they were
created at deep-sea vents. There is no
scientific agreement as to the origin of
cellular life. What we do know is that
all organisms are composed of one or
more cells, and virtually all cells
emerge from pre-existing cells.
Whether human, plant or animal, all
cells carry the information necessary
for regulating cell functions and
transmitting information to the next

generation of cells. The cell represents
potential, possibility and the dynamic
energy of life itself.

Your interaction with the surrounding world

The membrane that separates and
protects a cell from its surrounding
environment is similar to the outside
perimeter of the mandala. It enables
different molecules to pass into and
out of the cell. The membrane is said
to be 'semi-permeable', in that it can
either let a substance pass through
freely, pass through to a limited extent
or not pass through at all. Similarly, a
mandala is a dynamic living archetype
that changes as you interact with it.
It is in constant communication with
that which lies outside its perimeter.
And so it is with us human beings.

As you work with mandalas, the
concept of boundaries will become
more meaningful. If you consider

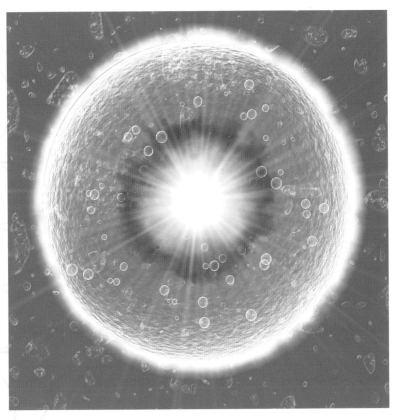

yourself and your life as a mandala, then you can choose who and what to let in, who and what can have limited access – or who and what can have none at all.

The perimeter of this radiant, mandala-like human egg cell has been permeated by a sperm cell, and now a new life has begun within.

The mandala in the garden

Perhaps the most beautiful mandala forms in nature are flowers. They symbolize romance and sexuality because of their delicate beauty, but also because they are the reproductive structure of flowering plants.

The flower mediates the union of male sperm with female ovum in order to produce seeds. The process begins with pollination and is followed by fertilization, which leads to the formation and eventual dispersal of the seeds. Flowers with brightly coloured petals and perfume-like scents attract insects that act as agents of pollination. The flower's function is to seduce. The flower is a powerful mandala form that symbolizes both the biological and the mystical power of sexuality.

Fruit and vegetable mandalas

The mandalic structure of the universe is also reflected by fruit and vegetables. Cut an apple or an orange in half and, before you enjoy it, study its intelligent mandala form. The segments of citrus fruit are especially beautiful and complex, while a mango has a strikingly erotic quality. Try this with any vegetable: cut it in half and study how it grew outward from a central point. Closely examine a cross-section of a green pepper, a bunch of celery or a marrow. There are many plant mandalas to observe and admire in the garden. The mandala form is everywhere among plants, and explains why the mandala is such a compelling and important vehicle for reconnecting to the natural world.

Tree mandalas

Perhaps the most touching mandala in the plant world is the tree mandala. If you examine a cross-section of a very old tree, you will have a glimpse into its life, not to mention into time itself. A tree produces a new ring each year, so by counting the rings you will know its age. The lighter parts of the rings show growth in the spring, while the darker parts represent growth in the late summer and autumn. If the tree had good growing conditions in a particular year, the ring will be fat. If the tree suffered from drought, the ring will be thin. The tree mandala represents courage, perseverance and wisdom. We can read the yearly 'rings' of our own life in a similar way and remember the courage with which we negotiated difficult times.

This gorgeous mandala-like Mammillaria cactus plant adorns itself with vibrant magenta flowers.

The mandala in the animal world

Many animals, spiders and insects reflect the circular, mandala nature of the universe. The sea urchin, the sea star, the sand dollar and the jellyfish all have circular bodies.

The jellyfish forms a graceful, translucent floating mandala as it moves through its home in the sea. Sand dollars are echinoderms, disc-shaped, spiny-skinned seabed animals that have five-part radial symmetry. Most sea stars also have five arms that radiate from a central disc. And the intelligent octopus takes on the form of a mandala. Octopuses have two eyes and four pairs of arms and, like other cephalopods, are bilaterally symmetric.

The spider and its web

On land, the spider with her centre and radiating appendages takes on a mandala shape, as does her web, although not all spiders spin webs in order to hunt prey. In numerous cultures, the origination of basket-weaving, knotwork, weaving, spinning and net-making has been attributed to the spider and her web. The spider is the central figure in many creation myths as she has the ability to shape her own environment by producing webs from her body.

The beautiful Sea Biscuit, or sand dollar, displays one of nature's most lovely mandalas.

Other animal mandalas

The structures that animals build are also often mandala-like. Consider the bird's nest – a carefully constructed, rounded container designed to receive the mother's eggs and then her baby birds after they hatch. Bits of twigs, moss and other dried matter are not haphazardly piled up, but are consciously shaped into a circular form. Bird, insect and reptile eggs function as both cell and mandala. Each egg contains the essence of another living being.

Animal horns, such as the curling horns of rams and the hooves of horses and deer, have rings that show their age. And turtles and fish have markings that reflect the cycles of time. The turtle is another beautiful example of the mandala in nature: possessing a rounded protective shell, powerful stubby legs and an ancient, wise head, it is believed in some indigenous cultures to support the world on its back. Other sea animals, such as the chambered nautilus, possess elegant and exquisitely beautiful spiral shells. The spiral is another mandala form that is frequently found in nature (see pages 44–45).

The Earth as mandala

Mandala patterns are found everywhere in geological form. Once you attune your eye, you will see them all over the natural world – in the shifting sand dunes of the desert, in the radiating patterns of crystals and in cone-shaped volcanoes with bowl-like craters.

The Earth was formed about 4.6 billion years ago, from matter produced by exploding stars. This matter, in the form of hot gases, eventually solidified into a sphere of molten minerals, which in turn cooled at the surface to form the crust upon which we live. On this relatively thin and fragile outer crust we still experience the eruption of the primeval fire that forms the centre of our planet. The energy of this primeval fire is sometimes violently released in volcanic eruptions – powerful forces that are capable of causing immense damage. From its fiery centre of molten hot lava to its perimeter at the Earth's crust, the planet we inhabit is itself a pulsating, breathing mandala. When we work with the mandala form, we connect with the Earth itself.

Because volcanoes vary in size from small undersea vents to huge mountains and volcanic 'fields', it is difficult to know how many there are. The Smithsonian Institution estimates that, during the past ten thousand years, about 1,300–1,500 land volcanoes have been active, and about 550 during recorded history. At present there are at least a thousand known magma systems that could erupt at any time. About 50–70 of those are active each year.

Crystal mandalas

Our planet also contains an amazing variety of crystals – ancient geological forms that offer especially beautiful displays of the mandala pattern in nature. Crystals were created as the Earth formed, and continue to change as the Earth changes. They are formed

This shockingly blue geode is a beautiful example of a crystal mandala.

from a variety of minerals and are defined by their internal structure. Each crystal has a unique geometric lattice that identifies it, created out of seven possible geometric forms: triangles, squares, rectangles, hexagons, rhomboids, parallelograms and trapeziums. Slicing a crystal in half reveals an exquisitely beautiful mandala.

Weather patterns as mandalas

As the Earth revolves around the sun, bands of hot and cold air collide.
These clashes can result in dangerous and violent weather patterns.
If the conditions are right, these patterns produce deadly rotating
hurricanes and tornadoes.

The revolving motion of the Earth itself produces these spiral and circular weather forms. A Doppler radar image of a hurricane shows Mother Nature in her most wrathful incarnation. We puzzle as to why such destruction exists, and why we have to live with these frightening natural mandalas. The quiet, still eye of the hurricane reminds us of the *bindu* of the Hindu mandala, the source of all creation. The mandala-like cloud formations rotating around the still centre of the hurricane represent the play of creation and destruction in the natural world.

Over land, thunderclouds can produce tornadoes. Under the right conditions, low pressure combined with strong updraughts creates funnel-shaped spinning vortexes that stretch from cloud formations to the ground. The violence of these whirling, dark columns of water and debris reminds us that life is both creative and destructive. Meditations on man-made mandalas from various

A hurricane circling around its centre – or eye – is a dynamic and powerful mandala form in nature.

spiritual traditions will also lead us to the same conclusion.

Snow and rain mandalas

Snow can be destructive or beautiful, or both. It all depends on the circumstances. But, without a doubt, the snowflake is one of the most magnificent mandala forms in nature. Snowflakes begin as water molecules that attach to particles of dust in the atmosphere, at freezing or below-freezing temperatures. When the snowflake gets heavy enough, it descends to Earth. Each snowflake is unique, and because of the way water molecules attach to each other, most are six-sided, or hexagonal. As the snowflake falls, it grows larger, creating an astonishingly beautiful and luminous mandala structure.

Finally, the raindrop, when it hits a body of water, creates concentric mandala forms. Circle upon overlapping circle radiates outward, reminding us of the dynamic quality of every aspect of life. Each raindrop that hits a body of water creates its own mandala. In a gentle rain, a pond's surface will become a sea of overlapping circles.

The body as mandala

When you look in the mirror in the morning, you may not see a mandala. But, on further reflection, you may come to understand how your physical body reflects the mandala principle.

The famous Italian artist Leonardo da Vinci (1452–1519) made that connection. His 'Vitruvian Man', a drawing that he completed in 1492, depicts the human body as a mandala. When drawn in this way – an image of a man in a circle, with his arms and legs outstretched – the body's navel appears at the centre of the circle. Leonardo understood the human being as the focal point of his or her own universe – the centre of the mandala – and the body itself as a representative of the mandala principle.

Striated windows into the soul

Humans begin life as a fertilized egg planted in the mandala of the mother's womb. There, our cells divide and multiply, radiating out to form an embryo. Our eyes are perhaps the most mandala-like aspect of our bodies. The iris – sometimes with visible radiating striations

moving outward from the dark pupil – forms a stunningly beautiful window into our souls.

Our life depends on the circulation of our blood and oxygen. The rhythmic beating of our hearts circulates our blood. We breathe in to bring oxygen into our lungs and around our bodies, and we breathe out to remove carbon dioxide. Through the cycles of our breath we are in constant exchange with the universe. The Ancients linked the breath to a life force. The terms 'spirit', *qi* and 'psyche' are related to the breath. The Hebrew Bible refers to God breathing the breath of life into clay to make Adam a living soul; it also describes the breath as returning to God when we die.

Like the Earth itself, we are a living, breathing, intelligent mandala, residing in the larger mandala of the universe.

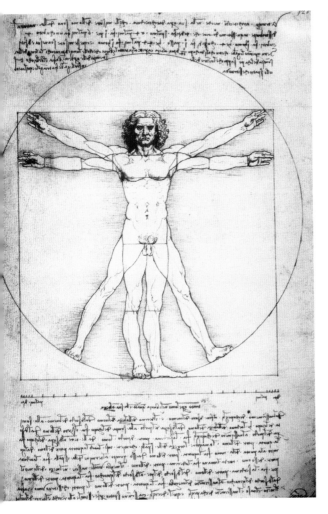

Leonardo da Vinci's 'Vitruvian Man' (c.1492) depicts the human body as a mandala.

The mandala of the life cycle

The circle of the mandala symbolizes nature's life cycles. The life cycle of a plant begins with a seed planted in earth. It grows, nurtured by the soil, the earth and the sun. Eventually it flowers, goes to seed and dies. The dead plant then fertilizes the earth, in which the new seed grows.

A plant grows, flowers, dies and then fertilizes the earth so a new seed can grow.

In our human life cycle we are born, mature into adulthood, live out our reproductive years and enter old age. Eventually our life comes to an end. It is the same in the animal world. But sometimes that full cycle is cut short. In the Buddhist and Hindu traditions, the life cycle ends in death, but comes full circle through reincarnation. The circle of the mandala reflects our own life cycle and those of the natural world. We are born in the centre and our lives radiate outward, and then, when we die, we return to the centre and the source, perhaps to be reborn.

The Triple Goddess

The Ancients were in tune with the life cycle or stages of life, which they expressed through devotion to various forms of the 'Triple Goddess'. The Greek goddesses Demeter, Persephone and Hecate represented the Maiden-

Mother-Crone archetype, as did the Hindu Triple Goddess, Saraswati, Lakshmi and Parvati. The Maiden represented birth and the promise of new beginnings – a time when a young woman embodies innocence and youthful enthusiasm. The Mother represented ripeness, fertility, sexuality and power, a time when she possesses awesome potential to give birth to another human being. Finally, the Crone embodied the wisdom that only comes with age and experience, and also represented death and endings.

The circular mandala form symbolizes the cycles of life from birth to death – and perhaps beyond. Every life cycle is connected to other cycles, forming an interconnected fabric of life. The mandala also represents a spiritual cycle of life: we are born in ignorance, through effort we develop spiritually and, if we are successful, we reach enlightenment – a state in which we meet God, merge with the One or achieve our Buddha-nature.

The Greek goddess Hecate, depicted as 'Hecate Triformis' – Virgin, Mother and Crone.

The mandala of time

If anything, the mandala form represents the cyclic nature of time. Our lives are measured in seconds, minutes, hours, days, weeks, months, years and, for some, decades. The sun rises and sets. If it is evening where you are, it is morning somewhere else in the world.

Because of its primordial nature, the mandala naturally brings up the issue of time. How long will you have to live? And what are you doing with your life? How are you using your precious and limited time on Earth? As you work with mandalas, these questions may arise, but the mandala provides a safe container in which to explore the answers that only you can provide.

Time can stretch or contract. It can 'fly by', when you are engrossed in what you are doing – when you are 'in the flow'. Or you may find yourself watching the movement of the second hand on the clock as you wait for the end of a boring meeting. If you find yourself in a deep meditative state, time will seem to expand and will perhaps cease to have any meaning. Time is never experienced in the same way from one moment to the next. The mandala will remind you that, while your personal life is finite, there is something beyond you that is timeless and infinite.

The Kalachakra mandala
In the Tibetan Buddhist tradition, there is a famous practice called Kalachakra, or the 'Wheel of Time'. Monks create the intricate Kalachakra mandala out of coloured sand as an aid to meditation. The meditation revolves around the concept of time (*kala*) and cycles (*chakra*), from the cycles of the planets to the cycles of human breathing. It teaches the practice of working with the most subtle energies within one's body on the path to enlightenment.

The mandala represents the cycles of time and the inevitability of death.

The mandala of the solar system

Within the spiral Milky Way galaxy lies our solar system, and then within our solar system lies Planet Earth. Each is a mandala that is part of a larger mandala.

From ancient times people were aware of the circular nature of the planets and stars. They turned to the sky above for direction and meaning. Their queries ranged from 'When shall I plant?' and 'When shall I hunt?' to 'Will the gods send rain?' They learned that the cycles of plants and animals, the timing of the first and last frost, and the beginning and end of seasons could be redicted by gazing at the stars and the sky. Sunrise, sunset, the phases of the moon, the annual appearance and disappearance of the constellations all occurred with undeviating and cyclical regularity.

Ancient peoples aligned their lives to the rising and setting of the sun.

Natural connections

People have used the sky as a guide to natural cycles since Paleolithic times. Alongside cave paintings of antelopes and bison are markings indicating the phases of the moon and the trajectory of the sun. The movement and position of the sun could be closely correlated with seasonal cycles of life,

These ancient cave paintings in California reveal a keen interest of our ancestors in the stars and planets.

and that of the moon with both the tides and women's menstrual cycles. So it is no wonder that the circle, or the mandala, has such symbolic power in the human psyche.

When we look up at the night sky, we witness daily astronomical events that we have come to take for granted. We live within a mandala so vast that it is beyond our comprehension. But making and colouring mandalas can help you reconnect with the cycles of life and provide you with much-needed healing energy.

The moon as mandala

The Earth's luminous white moon is one of the most stunningly beautiful mandala forms in nature. Like the mandala, the moon is not one-dimensional or static. Rather, it is a dynamic embodiment of the cyclical nature of time.

On average, the moon circles the Earth in about 29.5 days. The sun always illuminates the half of the moon facing it. When the sun and moon are on opposite sides of the Earth, the moon seems 'full' to us, and appears as a bright, round disc. When the moon is between the Earth and the sun, it appears dark, which we call a 'new' moon. In between those two phases, the moon's illuminated surface appears to grow (or 'wax') to full, then decrease (or 'wane') toward the next new moon. There are three major phases of the moon:

The new moon
In this phase, the moon is about to wax or grow. The moon appears 'dark' because the side of the moon that is being lit by the sun is not facing us. The new moon is a time for fresh beginnings and starting projects, such

as moving to a new house, taking a new job or beginning a new relationship. The mandala represents the potential of new beginnings.

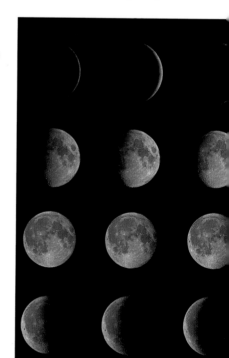

Waning moon

In this phase the moon is decreasing. This is a time of winding down, and of endings. If something is moving out of your life, you may notice the moon is in its waning phase. Meditate on the mandala to become more conscious of what is entering and leaving your life.

Full moon

In this phase the moon and its effect is at its most powerful. This is the time for healing, and the completion of projects. Colouring or meditating on a mandala will help you heal from illness and past psychic wounding.

The moon, one of the most stunning mandala forms in nature, is a potent symbol of the dynamic quality of life and the cyclical nature of time. As such, it offers endless opportunities for contemplation, meditation and reflection, and insight into the nature of the mandala itself.

A composite image shows the Moon at each stage of its 28-day cycle (a lunar month).

Exercise Tracking the cycles of the moon

It's sad to say, but many of us who live in cities rarely look at the moon. And because we fail to look up at the night sky, we forgo one of the most breathtakingly beautiful experiences of living on Earth.

We live so much indoors, moving from cars or public transportation to our homes or office buildings that we never take time to gaze at the stars. The night sky, especially, can be hidden by the glare of city lights. Finding a place to watch the moon in her phases, and tracking the moon's effect on your life, will help you reconnect with the rhythms, cycles and forms of nature, which are the basis of the mandala.

1 Commit to tracking the moon's phases for a month. Set aside a notebook or a computer file where, every day, you will record the phase of the moon and what you are currently experiencing in your life.

2 You can track the moon's phases by going outside every night, if the weather is clear, and looking up into the night sky. Or you can check online, or use a printed moon calendar. Some mobile phones have applications for following the moon's phases.

3 Each day briefly record the moon's phase, your emotional state and those events or experiences that were meaningful for you.

4 After a month has passed, go back and note if there are any interesting correlations or changes that you experienced when the moon was in her various phases. For example, did you begin any projects at the new moon? Did you end a project at the full moon or feel more restless than usual? When the moon was waning, did you have the feeling of winding down from a previous 'high'? If you are female, did you feel any connection with your menstrual cycle?

5 If you enjoy tracking the moon, continue to do so. If you do this, your relationship with the moon will deepen over time.

The moon and her tides

The moon, nature's most spectacular mandala form, has a powerful magnetic effect on ocean tides – yet another example of how the mandala draws its power and energy from nature.

The restless sea, with its swirling currents and swelling tides, has been the subject of art, music and mythology throughout time. Izanami, a Japanese goddess, was thought to control the tides. Hina-Ika, or 'Lady of the Fish', is a Hawaiian goddess related to the moon and tides. The English poet Geoffrey Chaucer (c.1342–1400) wrote, 'The sea desyreth naturally to folwen the moon.' And the Maoris tell of the goddess Rona, the 'Tide Controller'.

These mythic and literary examples express a reverence and respect for the moon's power. It is hardly a static white circle in the night sky; it is full of energy. The mandala form affects us so deeply because it embodies these aspects of nature and of the moon.

How do tides work?

When the tide is high, it is because the moon has pulled the ocean upward and outward, causing it to mound up. On the opposite side of the Earth from the moon, the Earth's rotation produces another mound of water and high tide. Between these mounded areas are flat areas, which we experience as low tides. Each day, with great regularity, the moon causes two high tides and two low tides.

As we have seen, the circular mandala form symbolizes the cosmic origin of life, but the moon as mandala may also point to our biological beginnings. Scientists suggest that the cyclical rise and fall of sea levels may have encouraged evolution. The moon's tides create a situation where life is exposed to both water and air within the space of a few hours. This alternation between two distinct ecological environments enabled sea organisms to get used to an alien environment before moving permanently to land.

The full moon, shown here over Canada's Vancouver Harbour, pulls at the ocean, causing the tides to rise and fall.

The circle in cultural expression

As a species, we organize ourselves into mandala-like communities and naturally gravitate to the centre. The local pub, the neighbourhood market, the school and the church serve as centres of our communities.

They underscore our need to gather together, to exchange goods, to share and to belong. They serve as magnets pulling us to the warmth, comfort and safety of the centre. Most cultures also have some kind of traditional circle dance, in which men, women and children face each other in a symbol of the Great Round. Children love to spin together on merry-go-rounds and play 'Ring a ring o' rosies'. We gather endlessly into what we refer to as 'circles': sewing circles, prayer circles, healing circles, reading circles and friendship circles. The 'social circle' suggests protection, equality, cooperation and inclusion, as well as the generation of energy for a specific purpose. The mandala in turn reflects community and rites of passage, and is a symbol of safety and home.

Social mandala forms

Humans have created mandala forms throughout history, from prehistoric stone circles, to Mayan observatories, to Rome's Pantheon – a perfectly

Rome's Parthenon, a perfectly round building built in 25 BCE to house statues of Roman gods and goddesses.

round building built in 25 BCE to house a circle of images of Roman gods and goddesses – and even the circular sports arena of today. Our gardens and public places often are designed as a circle, with streets or paths radiating outward. The circle eventually led to the wheel and, both literally and figuratively, drove us forward. For millennia we have instinctively created circles to mimic the great mandala of the universe and the circular forms and forces of nature.

Artists, healers and spiritual practitioners throughout time have gravitated to the circle. Hildegard of Bingen (1098–1179), a Benedictine abbess, painted exquisite mandala-like images depicting her mystical realizations, while Hindus and Buddhists continue the ancient practice of creating sacred mandalas in their respective traditions. Native American mandala-like sand paintings are used in healing rituals, and Navajo pottery and basketry frequently incorporate mandala-like designs. And the intricate knot patterns of the ancient Celts reflect a belief in the continuity of life and the interconnection of humans, plants, animals and the sacred.

The spiral as mandala

Spirals appear everywhere in the natural world, from spiral seashells to spiral-shaped plants, eddies and whirlpools. And spirals have always been a part of the human environment.

Somewhere around fifty thousand years ago our human ancestors began carving spiral shapes on rocks, reflecting the spirals in their environment. They made use of the spiral form in basket-weaving and coiled pottery.

Prehistoric humans knew the spiral as a symbol of creation, but also of entropy (disorder) and destruction. They observed that the spiral spins both ways in one continuous cycle. The yellow dandelion grows, then turns into a white puff, then explodes outward into oblivion; but in the spring, new dandelions emerge from the ground. Spiral-shaped seashells, abandoned by their inhabitants, are eventually ground into sand; but a new generation of sea animals uses the sand to build new shells. And spiral galaxies spin out and disappear into the void; but the gas and dust of the expired galaxies reconfigure and spin into new galactic forms.

The triple spiral

So it is no wonder that the 'triple spiral' is found carved at the entrance of sacred caves and burial grounds at Newgrange (see page 225), a megalithic burial mound and passage cave located in Ireland. The triple spiral is also found on a number of Neolithic sites, for example, on the Bugibba temple on Malta. And thousands of prehistoric sites scattered throughout the south-western United States, on cliffs, boulders and cave walls, are marked with spirals and other images incised in stone, which are known as 'petroglyphs'. Many of these sites were used as solar calendars to track the yearly movement of the sun across the sky, through the inter-play of sunlight on the petroglyph. From ancient times, the symbol of the spiral has been associated with the solar calendar, the rhythm of the seasons and the cycle of birth, death and rebirth.

The Maori people of New Zealand were also known to inscribe spiral tattoos on their faces and bodies, in order to make sure that in death their soul would be granted the 'vision of the spirits'.

Mutu, chief of the Ngaiterangi tribe, Bay of Plenty, New Zealand, c.1880, wears spiral tattoos on his face.

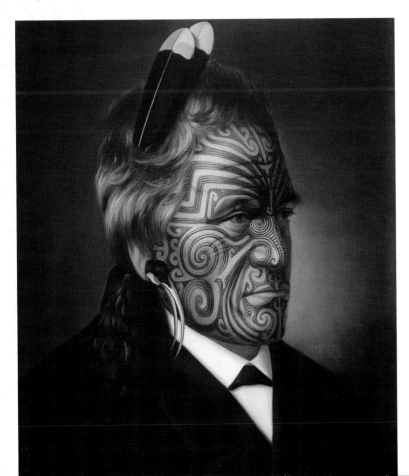

The circle in sacred architecture

Sacred architecture involves the marriage of the circle and the square, both of which are often combined in ancient man-made mandalas. The square is a human invention, whereas the circle represents the divine.

The integration of square and circle is expressed in the architecture of the church or temple. The cross and square determine the four cardinal directions (north, south, east and west), while the circle expresses the timeless, and dimensionless, centre of the universe. In the earliest cultures sacred places were identified by a circle and a cross, and related to the cardinal directions. The stone circle beneath the upside-down bowl-shaped sky gradually metamorphosed into the circular vaulted dome. And all over the ancient Mediterranean, from Turkey to Spain, the place of prayer was often a small cube with a hemispheric, mandala-like cupola above.

Native American architecture

While these circular architectural forms represented the bringing together of Heaven and Earth, in another part of the world the tent-pole remained a central symbol of the universal mandala. Native Americans constructed their medicine lodges with a central pole, which symbolized the centre of the world; 28 additional poles radiated outward and represented the days in the lunar month.

The square mandala of Vaishravana, a Tibetan Buddhist protector.

The mandala-like Hindu–Buddhist Borobudur Temple in Java, Indonesia.

These poles were placed so that they aligned with constellations sacred to the tribe. The Medicine Man would place the central pole at the intersection of four sacred directions or paths. The entrance to the lodge was placed to the east, the direction of the sunrise.

Hindu temple architecture

Hindus based their temples on a square mandala form, but one that was derived from the circle. A vertical post or pillar was put up, from which the sun cast its shadow. Around the post a circle was traced, and the shadow cast across that circle by the extremes of the sun's movement across the sky established the east–west axis. The circle then generated a square, and the four cardinal points were determined in relation to the altar. Therefore the square established the plan of the Hindu temple and its proportions. The cardinal axes offered a means of bringing together the circular Heaven and the terrestrial square.

Sacred dance and circumambulation

Many sacred dances take the form of the circle or mandala. For example, Hindu sacred dance is based on the god Shiva's fiery dance of destruction, in which he dances in a mandala of fire, destroying the ignorance that prevents enlightenment.

During Hindu sacred dance, the eyes follow the movements of the hands, and the feet establish the rhythm, which symbolizes the cycles of nature, and the need to dance in tune with the universe.

Sufi dervishes are practitioners of a mystical form of Islam, which focuses on love, being of service to others and transcending ego. Whirling is a Sufi form of meditation. It is a dance, performed as a spiritual practice, through which the dervish tries to transcend his ego and know divine perfection by listening to the music, meditating on God and spinning his body in repetitive circles. As he whirls, his arms are open. His right arm is raised to the sky, ready to receive God's blessings; his left hand is extended toward the Earth. He spins from right to left, with the intention of embracing all humanity with love.

Circumambulation
This is the act of physically moving around or circling a sacred object. Circumambulation of deity images or temples is an integral part of Hindu ritual. Buddhists circumambulate images of the Buddha, shrines or holy mountains, such as Mount Kailash in Tibet. In Islam, the same ritual is performed around the Kaaba in Mecca in a anti-clockwise direction. In the Catholic Church, a priest sometimes circumambulates the altar while carrying a metal censor suspended from chains in which incense is burned. And, at some Catholic shrines, it is the custom to circumambulate around an image of Mary, Christ or other sacred figure three times to honor the Holy Trinity.

A whirling dervish performing the Sema ceremony in Istanbul, Turkey.

The labyrinth as mandala

The labyrinth is a form of the mandala. Prehistoric labyrinths, which served as traps for malevolent spirits or as defined paths for ritual dances, appear throughout the world today. For example, there is a megalithic stone incised with a labyrinth near Pontevedra, Spain; and there are Celtic, Greek, Minoan, Etruscan and Babylonian labyrinths.

Theseus slays the Minotaur at the centre of the labyrinth.

The labyrinth gets its name from a Greek myth, in which the skilful artisan Daedalus built an elaborate structure – a labyrinth – for King Minos of Crete. He designed it to capture the Minotaur, a creature that was half-man and half-bull, which the hero Theseus would eventually kill. In order to capture the Minotaur, Daedalus made the labyrinth difficult to escape from. But the clever Ariadne provided Theseus with a ball of thread, enabling him to kill the Minotaur and find his way out again.

Spiritual associations

The labyrinth came to have additional spiritual meanings. Like other mandalas, it symbolizes the search for the One, or God, salvation or enlightenment. In medieval times the labyrinth symbolized the journey to

God – a path that leads along many deceptive twists and turns to the centre. The labyrinth also symbolizes the many dangers of the spiritual path: for example, one can get discouraged or lost in despair, or fall off the path altogether. But if these dangers are overcome, the centre awaits as a symbol of love and completion.

The best-known existing medieval labyrinth is inlaid in the floor of the Cathedral of Chartres. During the medieval era it would be walked as a pilgrimage or for repentance. As a pilgrimage, it was a questing, searching journey, with the hope of becoming closer to God. When used for repentance, the pilgrims would walk the path on their knees.

In the past few decades there has been a renewed interest in the labyrinth as a meditative tool (see pages 290–299). Many newly made labyrinths exist today, in churches and parks. Walking a labyrinth can help induce a contemplative state, as well as bring you closer to yourself and to your true nature.

The magnificent labyrinth mandala on the floor of the Notre Dame Cathedral, Chartres, France.

How to work with mandalas

Create your Mandala Journal

Before you begin, either buy or create a special blank book to be used as your Mandala Journal. Try to make your journal special, with a cover and binding that you find beautiful and meaningful. Decorate it, if you like, with images that please you – perhaps a coloured mandala from this book or one you created yourself.

Keep your Mandala Journal in a safe place, and try not to share it with others. It is a private journal and you need to feel free to write anything in it that you wish, without fear that others will read it and judge you.

Speaking through mandalas

Working with mandalas can be a very powerful and transformative spiritual process. You may find that, at times, words fail you and have trouble thinking through an issue in your life. But what eludes your thoughts or words may be illuminated in the images, colours and symbols of a mandala. And, to come full circle, you can deepen your mandala experience by returning to words, and writing about your insights and realizations in your Mandala Journal. You can record these immediately after completing a

mandala or later on, after it has had time to work on your psyche.

Acknowledging your shadow

At times what you write will be joyful and inspiring; at other times, as you work with your mandalas, you may unearth some difficult emotions. The mandala does not discriminate; it simply reveals what is truthful for you in that moment. What may seem negative could be your shadow emerging.

Your shadow is a powerful aspect of yourself, which you may have trouble acknowledging. It can be a negative aspect of yourself that you don't want to admit to, or a positive gift that you have yet to acknowledge or develop. A key to your shadow is that you may project it onto others. For example, you may find a fault

in other people that you are blind to in yourself; or you may admire someone who has a gift that you don't realize you yourself possess. In either case, your shadow is your 'gold', and it is worth mining it by means of the mandala process.

Record your mandala experiences in a journal to enhance your understanding and insight.

Colouring mandalas for pleasure, healing and transformation

Colouring mandalas evokes the pleasure that comes from working with universal, archetypal patterns of line and form, as well as promoting healing and spiritual transformation.

When they are coloured for healing purposes, mandalas can alleviate anxiety and fear, enabling your immune system to do its work. When coloured for personal or spiritual transformation, they help provide an awareness of the universe and the oneness of all life. There is something freeing about colouring mandalas. Their symmetry provides a soothing rhythm and predictability, which encourages a deep mental and physical relaxation. Your unique choices of colour, and the process of colouring itself, will cause something inside you to shift, and you will have discovered an excellent method for exploring and enhancing your life.

Colouring mandalas is a highly relaxing and pleasurable activity that can help you to deepen your awareness.

Connecting with your inner self

Colouring mandalas will connect you with nature and with the deepest parts of yourself. And, just as the content of the mandala emerges as you create it, so contemplating its meaning will further deepen your understanding. Meditating on your mandala will add a spiritual dimension to your process. As you focus on your completed mandala in all its beautiful detail and colour, you will discover its meaning and resonance. You may experience serenity, divine love, compassion, forgiveness, personal power or healing. Alternatively, you may uncover blocked emotions and suppressed memories that have been holding you back in your life. Whether you colour the mandalas that are provided in this book or create your own to colour, you will experience a connection with yourself, and with the world around you, at a depth you never previously thought possible.

THE BENEFITS OF COLOURING MANDALAS

Colouring mandalas can help you:

- Calm your mind
- Quieten your emotions
- Experience tranquillity and contentment
- Promote greater self-awareness
- Experience meditative states
- Reduce stress and anxiety
- Lower your blood pressure
- Heal yourself from illness
- Free yourself from addictions
- Promote a sense of well-being
- Ground and centre yourself
- Integrate different aspects of yourself
- Increase your ability to concentrate
- Stimulate your creativity
- Access your emotions
- Solve problems
- Feel satisfaction and pleasure
- Overcome emotional blocks
- Reach your full potential
- Access your higher wisdom.

How to colour the mandalas in this book

In the Mandala Workbook (see pages 304–85) is a collection of mandalas from the Hindu, Buddhist, Christian, Celtic and Native American traditions for you to colour. You can choose either to colour them in the book, or photocopy and enlarge them onto the paper of your choice.

Photocopying will enable you to use sturdier paper and a broader range of art materials, and give you the option to colour a particular mandala more than once. Before you begin working with the mandalas in this book you may wish to visit a photocopying shop and copy a selection of the mandalas in advance.

Coloured pencils

These are the easiest medium for colouring mandalas. When working with pencils, have a variety of erasers and smudge-tools handy, including a piece of leather chamois for shading. Shading from light to dark within segments of a mandala can create a subtle, three-dimensional effect. Solid colours will appear more jewel-like and, if chosen well, can also provide a

Coloured pencils, in a rainbow of different hues, are one of the best choices for colouring mandalas.

sense of dimension and depth. You will find an electric sharpener a great asset when working with coloured pencils.

Computer colouring

First, scan the mandala you want to colour into your computer, then open it in your favourite paint or drawing programme. Colour the mandala using solid, shaded or patterned colours. The benefit of using a computer is that you can make many versions of the same mandala and print them out larger or smaller than the original. You can then email your mandalas to friends, or print them out to give as gifts.

ART MATERIALS

Some materials you might consider using include:

- Coloured pencils
- Coloured markers
- Oil pastels
- Crayons
- Watercolours
- Gouache paint
- Acrylic paint

- A variety of papers on which to photocopy the mandalas.

Other items that you might require include:

- A palette, brushes and water jars, plus a protected work surface, if you are using paints
- An artist's portfolio in which to keep your completed mandalas
- Frames for the mandalas that you would like to display.

The meaning of colour in your mandalas

Colours have unique significance for each person. For example, you may have a childhood memory associated with the colour green. Because of that memory, you may be drawn to green or have an aversion to it.

Perhaps your childhood room was painted green when you really wanted it to be sky blue. Or you experience the colour green as hopeful and inspiring, because it reminds you of spring. Perhaps you have difficulty being in a yellow room because you find the colour too stimulating, or adore lavender because it was your beloved grandmother's favourite hue. If you have a strong positive or negative reaction to a colour you may want to do a little emotional digging to understand its source. Pay particular attention to your thoughts and feelings when this colour shows up in a mandala that you are working on, and see what you discover about yourself.

In addition to our personal colour preferences, we have inherited cultural associations for colour that are often deeply rooted in our psyche. Colour symbolism is a vast topic, but the following text offers a small taste to get you thinking about your colour choices as you work with mandalas.

Black

Black lacks hue and brightness; it absorbs light without reflecting any of its rays. It can produce a feeling of formality, and is often the colour of authority and power. Black is associated with evil, mystery and darkness. It symbolizes the nefarious, the horrible and the treacherous, as well as death. In many cultures, black is the colour of mourning. Yet black is also associated with birth, the womb and the creation of the universe.

Black can symbolize endings, but also the beginning of a process.

In Western psychology our shadow represents those aspects of ourselves that we would rather not confront.

Darkness is the place of germination, and black is the colour of origination and beginnings. Our ancient ancestors chose caves and dark spaces for celebrations of fertility dedicated to the great mother goddesses. New life emerges from the darkness of the womb, and seeds gestate in the darkness of the soil. Black is simultaneously empty and fecund. Ancient goddesses presided over the mystery of birth in which new life emerges out of darkness. No wonder the Greek goddess Diana of Ephesus was depicted with a dark face and hands. The Black Madonnas of Catholic Europe are perhaps a continuation of the mystery of the black goddess.

Black is also a symbol of what cannot be seen, and what lies beyond our awareness. It symbolizes the unconscious. We fear being taken over by the unknown forces in our unconscious and we project that fear outside of us, as a scary monster or frightening evil creature that dwells in the dark of night. Hence we love horror movies, where we can sit in the dark and be scared, knowing that the 'monsters' inside us (those aspects of ourselves that we reject and fear) are safely projected out there on the cinema screen.

In Western psychology our shadow represents those aspects of ourselves that we would rather not confront – our selfishness, our desire, our greed, our jealousy, our anger and other destructive qualities that threaten to overwhelm us – as well as those positive gifts that we are afraid to acknowledge and develop.

Black represents a turning in on oneself. A preponderance of black in your mandalas may signal depression. but that 'dark night of the soul' – if worked through with consciousness – can lead to new understanding, and to personal and spiritual transformation. The process of integrating the material in our unconscious into our conscious ego can reward us with psychological maturation. Through colouring and creating mandalas we have a safe container in which to explore that which is dark in us, and those things that we fear knowing, as well as our gifts that we have neglected to develop. We can also give birth, out of a dark space, to a new phase of our life.

White

The colour white is without hue and lies opposite black on the colour wheel. Whereas black does not reflect light, white reflects the light of all hues. White light, when passed through a prism, expands into the full spectrum of all colours. White can signify both the absence of colour or the sum of all colours. The colour white is a symbol found in the creation stories of many cultures and

The Tibetan Buddhist White Tara, known as the 'mother of liberation', embodies compassion, healing power and serenity.

represents the birth of consciousness. In the spiritual realm, white represents the radiant, infinite consciousness of the divine. Jesus said, 'I am the light of the world.' For Buddhists, the colour white symbolizes the seed of Buddha-nature within us. And in the Tibetan Buddhist tradition the female

Buddha White Tara is said to be the embodiment of compassion.

White is a symbol of the spiritual, and of the non-material and otherworldly realms that transcend our ordinary reality. It represents purity, innocence, fairness and virginity. White is the colour of innocence and childhood. It can also represent sterility, as the sterile feel of an all-white room is lacking the warmth of colour. An overabundance of white can feel like death. Indeed in some cultures, such as Japanese culture, white represents death and is worn for mourning. White is the colour of the shroud and of ghosts.

White is also the colour of passage, symbolizing death and rebirth. It is the colour of initiation and 'rites of passage'. Young black African men smear their bodies with a matt chalk white during initiation to show that they are, for the moment, outside society. White is also the colour of the East, and of first light, the moment of void between day and night, when we are still bound up in the world of dreams. If white shows up in your mandalas, it may signal that you are in transition in your life.

In nature, white is the colour of the moon and the stars. It is also the colour of milk, bone and semen. An ancient creation story from Egypt attributes the beginning of time to the ejaculation of a male god. And vast lakes of milk are part of the creation stories of Central Asia, recalling the nurturing abundance of the mother.

In alchemy, white was the colour of purification. It represented the act of stripping oneself of what was no longer needed, in order to prepare for a higher level of consciousness. In dreams white may symbolize new beginnings. And in the Christian faith white is the colour of Easter, signifying the resurrection of Christ and the triumph of the spirit over death.

Red

Red is the primary colour at one extreme end of the visible spectrum. The colour red can increase your pulse rate and breathing and cause your blood pressure to rise. Infants and children respond well to red.

A Chinese bride wears a traditional red wedding dress, a colour associated with love.

A medieval executioner, shown here brandishing the head of this victim, wears red, a colour associated with death.

This colour is also said to be for the amorous, the outspoken and the optimistic. Red can make you hungry by increasing your body's metabolism, and restaurants use red for this reason. It also symbolizes fire, heat, passion, urgency and danger. Red is the colour of blood and fire, and is associated with warmth and power. As a symbol of life, red can represent healing.

The colour red is also associated with death. The medieval executioner and blacksmith dressed in dark red. Both handled the essence of life – one in the form of blood and the other in the form of molten metal. Red ochre was used in ancient cave paintings, rituals and burial chambers. Its presence in Neolithic graves may have been to help the dead in the after-life. The shaman, the spiritual leader of a tribe, often painted himself with red ochre. And for the Anglo-Saxons red was considered protective and magical. They painted trees and weapons red to protect against evil, and to imbue their warriors with magical powers.

Red is the colour of love and has been used to suggest energy, passion and the erotic in Indian and Western cultures. In ancient Rome, brides wore a red veil – a custom still practised today in parts of Greece, Albania and Armenia. In China, the wedding gown and veil are red.

In its most positive sense, red is the colour for courage, strength and a pioneering spirit. In Japan, red is a symbol of true-heartedness and good luck. In the Shinto religion, red denotes harmony and expansiveness. In India, red is associated with the feminine divine. Many of the Hindu goddesses of India are depicted wearing red, representing the principle of creation and activity. However, in its most negative aspect, red is the colour of anger, violence and brutality. We talk about 'seeing red' when describing extreme anger.

Dark red is related to the womb. It is the colour of the soul and the heart. It is also the colour of knowledge, especially hidden or forbidden knowledge that is meant only for the initiated. Red in your mandalas can mean many different things. The best way to understand it is to read it in the context of other colours and forms in your mandalas.

Blue

Blue is the primary colour between green and violet in the visible spectrum. It can be a calming, soothing colour and, in neurological tests, the brain relaxes in response to blue. Contemplating this colour can lower the blood pressure and slow the pulse and respiration. Blue is associated with the sky, water, coolness and shadows. It suggests peace, tranquillity and serenity. It relates to the throat and is associated with self-expression, speech, communication and the ability to convey one's needs to others. Blue is the colour of responsibility, trustworthiness and compassion – meanings that are especially attached to royal blue.

Blue represents the spirit of truth and purpose. The Egyptians used this colour to symbolize truth. Blue is also an attribute of Jupiter and Juno, the Roman god and goddess of Heaven. The Indian god Vishnu has blue skin, indicating his all-pervasive nature; Krishna, an incarnation of Vishnu, also has blue skin and is depicted as a

The Hindu god Krishna, and his friend and lover Radha, rest on the belly of Kailya, a poisonous snake.

young, playful man in a relaxed pose. For Tibetan Buddhists, blue is the colour of *vairocana* or transcendent wisdom. It is the colour of emptiness, which is often symbolized in that tradition as a vast blue sky. Blue light is what opens one to liberation.

In many cultures, blue indicates religious feeling, devotion and innocence. It represents the vertical and spatial, and refers to height and depth, as in the blue sky above and the blue sea below. Lapis lazuli is a semi-precious stone that has

Jodhpur, India, is known as 'The Blue City', because many houses around the city's Mehrangarh Fort are painted blue.

been valued since ancient times for its intense blue. In the Egyptian Book of the Dead lapis lazuli – made in the shape of an eye set in gold – was considered one of the most powerful amulets. Blue lapis lazuli is said to open the 'third eye' and bring enlightenment.

Very dark shades of blue, such as indigo, can represent terrorizing aspects of the mother archetype and, in your mandalas, a difficult relationship with your earthly mother. The Indian goddess Kali is shown with very dark-blue skin; she represents the mother as both the giver of life and its destroyer, the womb and the tomb. Dark indigo can also represent the overwhelming enormity and power of nature.

Blue is also the colour of infinity. Light blue is the hue of imagination, while dark blue is the hue of dreams. Light blue – the light of the day and consciousness – eventually gives way to midnight blue, the colour of dreams.

Yellow

Yellow is the primary colour that lies between green and orange in the visible spectrum. It is the hottest, most expansive and burning of all the colours in its intensity. It is the colour of youth, strength and male divinity. The yellow of the sun's rays searing across the blue sky displayed to the ancient peoples of the Earth the power of the gods. Sun worship was one of the most widely practised forms of devotion in ancient times, and the colour yellow was associated

with solar deities such as the Greek god Apollo and the Egyptian sun god Ra. In Native American traditions, yellow was associated with wisdom and the ability to actualize your higher self in the world. On medicine wheels (see page 234) yellow was the colour of the East and represented

This detail from the inner coffin of Nespawershefi shows the Egyptian sun god Ra against a solar yellow background.

wearing yellow clothes. Yellow can also have negative effects – babies cry more often and longer in yellow rooms, and in convalescent homes it can make older people shake, as it affects their movement. For some people this colour can induce feelings of anxiety or anger. Yellow is both powerful and complicated in its meanings. It symbolizes cowardice, caution and fear, as well as warmth, energy and brightness. Because of its association with the sun and its light, yellow symbolizes being able to see and understand. It also represents consciousness, individuality and the imagination. Intuition is related to the colour yellow, as is the ability to be autonomous.

In Jungian psychology, yellow suggests the masculine and the father. For women, yellow is a symbol of their animus, or the active aspect of their nature. For both men and women, this colour is related to being active, self-supporting, independent and forward-thinking. In astrology,

illumination and the ability to see things clearly.

Yellow is the colour of egg yolk and ripe lemons. It is the hue of a sunny disposition and the idealist. But yellow is also associated with violence, envy, greed and treachery. Judas Iscariot is often portrayed yellow is associated with the sun sign Leo. If yellow appears in your mandalas you may be embarking on a more active, autonomous phase of your life.

Yellow represents the precious metal gold, which itself symbolizes riches, both material and spiritual. Gold can symbolize the gold within you, and your potential for developing an integrated and whole self.

Green

Green is the secondary colour between yellow and blue in the spectrum. A mixture of blue and yellow creates green, which is Mother Nature's colour. It is the hue of most live grasses and leaves, of some fruits while ripening and of the sea. In Celtic myth the Green Man – a mythical man with a face covered with leaves – is the god of fertility. Green is the universal symbol of nature and freshness and is associated with transitions. It also symbolizes health, regeneration, contentment, harmony and friendship. Green is a

Green is the colour of nature, hope, growth and spiritual renewal.

comforting colour that brings hope and good cheer. It is the colour of the awakening of life after a long, lonely winter. If green appears in your mandalas it may signal a time of renewal after a difficult period in your life.

For Native Americans, green symbolized innocence, being close to nature, trust and keen senses. It represents the ability to cherish and accept others as they are. For the mystic, Hildegard of Bingen, green represented God as dwelling in the Earth. Celtic mythology is populated with green-coloured creatures such as water sprites, wood nymphs and fairies, which survived from older earth-centred religions. In Islam, green is the most important colour and represents both paradise and spiritual renewal.

According to Juan Eduardo Cirlot, author of *A Dictionary of Symbols*, green relates to the goddess Venus and to nature, and symbolizes sympathy and adaptability. Green

Buddhist monks wear orange robes to signify their renunciation of ordinary life and their connection to the Buddha.

is the colour of earthy, tangible, immediately perceptible growing things and represents the function of 'sensation'. But Cirlot also associates green with death. It is both the colour of the bud and of decay. And the Egyptians painted Osiris – the god of vegetation and of the dead – green.

Green has its associations with negativity. For example, the poisonous venom of a snake is green. There is also the common phrase 'being green with envy'. But most people have a positive relationship with this colour, as it universally suggests freshness, harmony, nature and renewal.

Orange

Orange is the secondary colour between red and yellow in the spectrum, formed by the mixture of red and yellow pigments. As such, it represents the midway point between the red of libido and the yellow of spirit. In India, orange is the colour of the sacral chakra (see page 93), which rules sexuality and emotional relatedness. It is also the colour of the velvet cross of the Knights of the Holy Ghost, a Catholic order of chivalry under the French monarchy, founded in 1578. Because it is difficult to maintain a balance between sexuality and spirituality, orange often symbolizes lust and infidelity. If this colour appears in your mandalas you may be struggling with balance between your animal instincts and the higher aspects of yourself.

Orange also symbolizes confidence, creativity, adventurousness and sociability. It is the colour associated with the autumn and the harvest, when pumpkins ripen and the leaves turn many colours. It evokes warmth and happiness, and the glow of the fire. But it also evokes the cycles of life that include death. Autumn is the time of Halloween, the Day of the Dead festivals in Latin America, the celebration of Samhain in the pagan traditions and the Obon festival in Japan. These cultural events reflect that harvest time was the end of a cycle. The colour orange, so prominent in the autumn, evokes entropy and the inevitable deterioration of all things.

Orange is also the hue of the outcast. In India, criminals wore the colour orange, as prisoners in America still do today. But it is through this feeling of being an outcast – rejected and alienated – that one can deepen one's spiritual understanding. The Buddha, once a wealthy prince, left behind the pleasures of his father's home in order to find enlightenment; he became a voluntary outcast and donned orange robes to signify his renunciation. To this day many Buddhist nuns and monks wear orange robes.

Orange can also symbolize power. In its positive aspect, it can suggest a strong sense of identity and the ability to assert oneself in a good way. In its negative aspect, it can symbolize the ego-centred use of power and a lack of self-discipline.

Purple/violet

Purple and violet are colours mixed from red and blue. They are the colours of fantasy and suggest magical relationships, intimacy and sensitivity. Young girls like their rooms painted a shade of purple or violet. Boys find these colours too feminine.

But in the grown-up world, purple is above all associated with royalty, wealth and sophistication. It suggests high rank, and is the sign of authority.

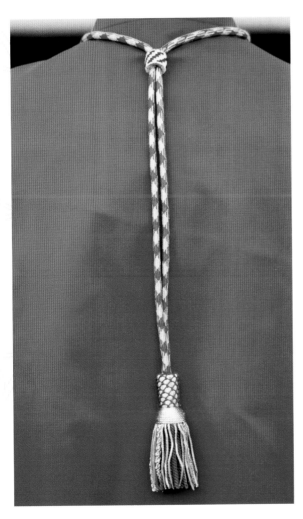

A priest's purple robe suggests the cooling of passion by spiritual aspiration.

In the West, purple dye was the most expensive to produce, as it was made from rare molluscs, so only the rich could afford purple garments. Byzantine and Roman emperors, for example, wore purple robes.

In China, the common English name of the imperial palace compound in Beijing is 'The Forbidden City', but this is a translation of the Chinese name Zijin Cheng, which literally means 'Purple Forbidden City'. In Chinese lore, purple was the colour of the North Star, which was considered the centre of Heaven and the site of the 'Purple Palace' of the heavenly emperor; the Forbidden City was considered the earthly emperor's 'Purple Palace'.

In the Christian tradition, bishops wear purple. The combination of red (which represents energy) and blue

The colour lavender represents mystical experience, spiritual awakenings and positive spiritual development.

(which represents spirituality) suggests the cooling of passion by spiritual aspiration. If purple appears in your mandalas you may be opening up to spiritual experience. Churches are decorated with purple during Lent, a time of self-deprivation and penance designed to strengthen one's ties to God. Christ is shown in a purple robe when he is depicted as suffering through his passion.

Purple also symbolizes intelligence and creativity, and the positive use of the imagination. It is associated with temperance, clarity of mind, deliberate action and the balance between Heaven and Earth. Violet is the colour of appeasement, in that the fire of red is softened. Purple and violet, in their negative manifestations, can suggest certain psychological imbalances, such as narcissism and authoritarianism.

Lavender

Like the colours purple and violet, lavender is mixed from red and blue, but with the addition of white to produce a lighter shade. Although it is lighter than purple, lavender has an intensity all of its own, and has a special, almost sacred place in nature: lavender, orchid, lilac and violet flowers are delicate and considered to be precious. If lavender appears in your mandalas it could suggest something unique or special appearing in your life.

Lavender and yellow symbolizes the holy day of Easter in the Christian religion, because Easter occurs in spring when the crocus flower, which

is lavender and yellow, blooms in Europe. In Buddhism, the aura of the Buddha is believed to be *prabashvara*, a shade of lavender. Lavender is also associated with mystical experience, awakening of the spirit, and positive spiritual development. On the other hand, this hue can also represent a state of being ungrounded and unconnected to reality.

Lavender is associated with the Olympian god Mercury, who was thought to rule the nervous system. And essential oil of lavender is known to have a calming effect on the nervous system.

Pink

Pink is mixed from red and white. It is associated with the feminine: girl babies often wear pink, as do older female children. Though the colour pink has sometimes been associated with feminine stereotypes, some feminists claim it as their own. The American activist women's group Code Pink uses it as their colour. Because pink is so strongly associated with femininity, the pink ribbon is the international symbol of breast-cancer awareness. In Jungian psychology,

pink appearing in a mandala is a symbol of the feminine, whether it appears for men or women. In Japan, however, the colour pink is considered masculine. The pink blossoms of cherry trees represent the young Samurai warriors who died in the prime of life.

Pink is associated with the body. It is the colour of flesh, sensuality

Pink is associated with the body, flesh, sensuality and the emotions.

and the emotions. According to Juan Eduardo Cirlot, the Gnostics associated pink with the Resurrection of Christ. Pink recalls the suffering of being human, of dealing with the physical and emotional pain associated with being in a body, of having flesh, muscles, organs and tissue. Pink symbolizes vulnerability and the need for self-care. If pink appears in your

mandalas you may need to give yourself permission to take better care of yourself: to learn to reduce stress through relaxation, to eat healthier foods and to get more exercise. You may also need to open up to others and ask for the help you require. Pink is considered the colour of good health – we speak of feeling 'in the pink' or of feeling as fresh as a newborn babe.

Peach

To create the colour peach, you add a bit of yellow to the colour pink. It is a more adult version of pink, suggestive of sexuality as well as sensuality. The colour peach symbolizes strength, protection, confidence and the speaking of truth. It can also suggest good health or something that is experienced as quite wonderful. The colour peach can be friendly and more soothing than its brighter and redder cousin orange, yet still retains its energy. In your mandala, the colour peach can symbolize empathy and harmony as expressed by a counsellor or therapist figure. It can also suggest the return of good health after a bout of illness, symbolize an aspect of you that is gentle and kind or a desire for a sensuous experience.

In China, the peach was a symbol of longevity, female sexuality, purity and truth. A peach with its leaf attached signifies the union of the heart and tongue, or 'truth'. The peach was a symbol of the female genitalia in Taoist sexual mysticism and regarded as the source of the ambrosia of life, which gave gods

The colour peach is symbolic of longevity and immortality, as well as beauty and love.

their immortality. According to Barbara G. Walker, author of *The Woman's Encyclopedia of Myths and Secrets*, peach blossom referred to a virgin in Taoist symbolism, while the fruit stood for a mature woman whose juices were essential to men's health. The colour peach in your mandala can reflect these ancient meanings of the fruit and its blossom.

The peach also represented the vulva and marriage in European symbolism. The Romans associated the fruit with Venus, the goddess of beauty and love. And in medieval times the peach was believed to be an aphrodisiac, and the colour peach may symbolize the same, if it appears in your mandala.

In Taoist mythology, the god Yu Huang (also called the Jade Emperor) and his mother Xi Wangmu (also known as the Queen Mother of the West) are said to be the guardians of the peaches of immortality. Xi Wangmu's attendants are depicted holding three peaches, and Zhang

Guo, one of the Eight Chinese Immortals, is often depicted carrying a peach. It was understood that simply eating the peaches of immortality did not, in itself, confer immortality. One had to live a virtuous life, eat a vegan diet and practise meditation.

The colour peach appearing in your mandalas may signal a transformative sexual relationship.

Magenta

Magenta is a deep purplish-red that is created in painting by adding red to an existing purple colour. Another name for magenta is fuchsia, after the fuchsia plant, which is known for its purple-red flowers. Some people argue that magenta does not exist. Sir Isaac Newton fed white light through prisms and discovered that magenta did not show up in the spectrum of colours, but when he superimposed the red end of the spectrum onto the blue end, he saw the colour magenta. So this is the only colour that does not

The colour magenta suggests modernity, vitality, restlessness and the dominance of the mind.

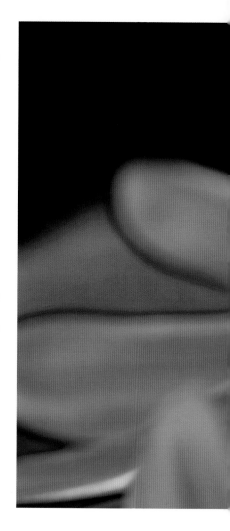

exist in a single wavelength. This underscores the fact that colour is a function of light, is dependent on the brain and is only experienced in the mind.

The colour magenta is a new colour in the history of humans. The purple-red dye magenta is a synthetic dye, first produced commercially in France in 1858. It was called 'fuchsine' after the fuchsia plant, but was soon named 'magenta' after the town in northern Italy where the French defeated the Austrians in 1859. The chemical giant Ciba-Geigy was established for the purpose of manufacturing magenta dye.

Magenta suggests modernity, vitality, restlessness and the dominance of the mind. It represents a vivacity that the shy or timid may find unnerving to be around. It is not an earthly colour, but rather one created in the laboratory. It can make a dramatic, bold statement when worn in articles of clothing, suggesting self-confidence, creativity and individualism. Magenta can suggest a break with tradition and a refusal to accept societal expectations, especially if you are a woman.

Brown can be found everywhere in nature. It is the colour of tree bark, soil, animal fur, human hair and skin.

The positive meanings of magenta in your mandalas include the ability to learn, and initiate and form opinions. On the negative side, magenta may mean a kind of self-centred, aggressive individualism in which you lose connection with others.

Brown

To create the colour brown, mix one primary colour with its complementary colour. For example, red and green are complementary colours, so when you mix them together you get brown. Or you can add one secondary colour to two primary colours. For instance, try mixing yellow and blue paints to make green. Add red paint to that green to make brown.

The colour brown is abundant in nature. Many soils are brown, as are animal furs, bird feathers, insects, human hair and human skin. Many types of wood and the bark of numerous trees are brown. This colour can be sad and wistful, like that of an empty field or trees with

dry leaves in late autumn. The colour brown is the hue of melancholy.

Faeces are usually brown, so this colour can be associated with excrement and waste – that which is natural, but considered dirty and unpleasant. Brown in your mandalas can be a statement of low self-esteem and a sense of worthlessness. If your life seems filled with waste – wasted time, money, relationships and opportunity – rest assured that there is hope. From soil fertilized with waste, new growth emerges. That inside you that you feel is unpleasant, and which you have rejected, may be your gold.

Brown suggests the earth and simplicity. It is trustworthy and solid. For the Catholic Church, brown was the symbol of humility and the vow of poverty, which is why some orders of monks wore a brown hooded robe made of rough cloth. St. Francis of Assisi chose a brown robe as the garb of the Franciscan order.

In its negative associations, brown can suggest the underworld and war. For example, the colour brown is associated with Nazi Germany and the Second World War.

Turquoise

To create the colour turquoise you must mix together blue and green. Your turquoise may be more green or more blue, depending on your proportions. Turquoise is sometimes called 'aquamarine'. In the visible spectrum, the transition between green and blue can appear to be blue-green or turquoise.

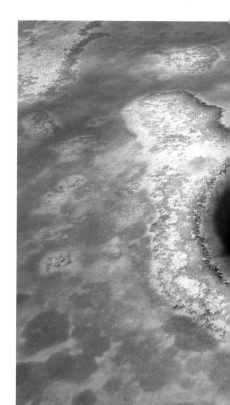

The colour turquoise comes from the opaque blue-green mineral of the same name, which was esteemed for thousands of years as a sacred stone and talisman. The burial mask of Tutankhamun was heavily inlaid with turquoise. Ancient Persians wore a turquoise stone as an amulet for protection against untimely death; if the stone changed colour, it was a warning of danger or infidelity. In the Middle East, turquoise is used to ward off the evil eye. And wearing turquoise was often believed to ensure prosperity. As a healing stone, turquoise supports the assimilation of nutrients – when placed on a horse's bridle it was said to prevent accidents and falls. For Native Americans, turquoise was a symbol of prosperity

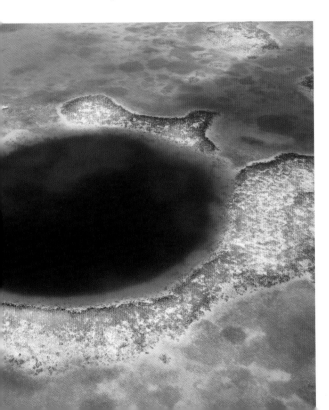

Turquoise is the colour of compassion, healing and higher spiritual dimensions.

and positive attitude. Because of this it was said to scare away evil spirits.

In Tibetan Buddhist prayers and literature, the word for turquoise is used to describe natural objects such as lakes, wells and flowers. Tibetans and other Himalayan peoples value turquoise for its mystical, religious and healing powers. Tibetan children are always given a piece of turquoise to keep them from falling.

Turquoise is the colour of compassion and healing, and both the stone and the colour encourage inner healing through its ability to enhance empathy and caring. It is also associated with the thymus gland and the immune system. Turquoise can help to balance personalities that are excessively polarized or un-balanced. It can assist you in attuning to a higher spiritual dimension or order. The colour turquoise represents the highest form of understanding, and facilitates giving and receiving. It also enhances intuition and spiritual growth. If the colour turquoise appears in your mandalas, it may mean that your health, your spiritual life and/or your emotions require your focused attention.

Grey

Grey describes the colours ranging from black to white. These are neutral hues with a low colour content. Some greys are monochromatic, with absolutely no hint of colour; others have a cool or warm cast, ranging from hints of blue or purple to browns and reds. In nature, grey suggests ashes, stone or an overcast sky. In many cultures stones have sacred, magical qualities. Stone circles in the Celtic tradition define sacred space, while Japanese and Chinese gardens use stones as sacred objects.

In a Japanese garden, grey gravel, which represents the waves and currents of water, is raked around carefully placed stones, which represent islands. The grey-coloured, constructed landscape invites contemplation and quiets the mind.

The colour grey in mandalas can symbolize depression, ageing or a lack of emotion. Alternatively, it can suggest that you have arrived in a calm, peaceful place after much emotional turmoil. Grey may also suggest that you are cutting off your emotions or feeling guilt for being your authentic self. In the Christian

tradition, grey is associated with Lent and atonement. During the Middle Ages people wore sackcloth and ashes to do penance for wrongdoing. Grey is also associated with the wisdom of age and the ability to understand that nothing is black or white but, rather, is composed of shades of grey.

Raked gravel in a Zen garden represents swirling water and the passage of time.

Chinese and Hindu colour symbolism

The meridians or energy pathways used in traditional Chinese medicine and the Hindu chakra system make extensive use of colour symbolism. Try applying these colour correspondences to your mandalas to gain insight about yourself and to help reconnect your body, mind and spirit.

Meridians are pathways in traditional Chinese medicine that carry 'chi', or vital energy, throughout the body. There are five main pathways that are mirrored on our right and left sides. In diagnosing a patient, a Chinese doctor will often look for a subtle hue emanating from the face, to determine which meridian system is out of balance.

MERIDIANS AND THEIR ASSOCIATED COLOURS AND EMOTIONS

Meridian	Element	Colour	Emotion	Imbalance
Lung/large intestine	Metal	White	Grief	Difficulty taking in and letting go
Stomach/spleen	Earth	Yellow	Worry	Poor digestion, lack of nurturing
Heart/small intestine	Fire	Red	Excessive laughter, mania	Difficulty with self-analysis and communication
Bladder/kidney	Water	Indigo or black	Fear	Low energy and libido
Liver/gall bladder	Wood	Green	Anger	Overwork and stubbornness

CHAKRAS AND THEIR ASSOCIATED COLOURS AND SPIRITUAL LESSONS

Chakra (*Sanskrit* name)	Location	Colour	What it governs	Spiritual lesson
Root (*Muladhara*)	Base of the spine	Red	Will to live, connection to body and the physical plane	How to function in the material world
Sacral (*Svadistana*)	Just below the navel	Orange	Emotions; sexuality	Manifestation in the world
Solar plexus (*Manipura*)	Between the navel and ribcage	Yellow	Personal power; autonomy	Love of self
Heart (*Anahata*)	Heart	Green	Love; integration of mind/body and male/female energies	Love and compassion for others; trust
Throat (*Vishuddha*)	Throat	Turquoise	Communication and creativity	Truthfulness
Third eye (*Ajna*)	One finger above and between the eyebrows	Indigo	Creative thought and wisdom	Understanding reality and detachment
Crown (*Sahasrara*)	Top of head in the centre of the skull	Violet	Connection with the divine; spirituality; universal energy	Living in the now; surrender

The Hindu chakra system

The word *chakra* means 'wheel' in Sanskrit. Yoga identifies seven of these wheels, or hubs of energy, that are vertically aligned along the spine. The chakras are often depicted as lotuses, whose petals open as spiritual energy and consciousness travel from the base of the spine to the crown of the head. Each chakra has a corresponding colour, parts of the body it governs and a spiritual lesson it imparts.

Creating a sacred space for working with mandalas

Colouring mandalas is an enjoyable pastime, and it is fine to colour them whenever you feel like it – perhaps when you are watching television. However, more profound benefits await you if you bring focus and intention to the colouring or mandala-making process.

One way of bringing intention to what you do is to create a sacred space – somewhere that is devoted to your personal or spiritual transformation. Creating a sacred space for working with mandalas will help you reap greater benefits from the process.

Are you attracted to the idea of having your own sacred space and excited about the prospect of creating one? Or do you feel, for some reason, that you don't deserve to have one? If you feel self-conscious or undeserving, ask yourself why this is so? Giving yourself the time and space to contemplate your deepest

Creating your own sacred space is a way of validating yourself and your need for personal time.

needs, and to develop emotionally and spiritually by working with mandalas, is one of the best gifts you can give yourself. Working with mandalas will help you build your capacity to love yourself and others, and to shed any feelings of unworthiness you may have.

Evoking a sense of the sacred

Your sacred space can be temporary – a favourite comfortable chair to sit in when you colour with your pencils – or a separate room with a drawing table, if you are using a broader range of art materials. You can add items to your space that evoke the sacred. It could be a candle, an image or figure of a divine being, or a symbol of

Dedicating a sacred space to working on mandalas and filling it with inspirational objects will fuel your creativity.

nature such as a crystal, a beautiful shell or fresh flowers. You may want room to hang up your completed mandalas. Burning incense or listening to meditative music can help invoke a sense of sacred space.

When using this space for colouring mandalas it is best to set aside at least an hour when you can be alone and undisturbed; if possible, finish colouring a mandala in one sitting. You can spend additional time contemplating your mandala, or you can put it away and come back to it at a later date.

Colouring mandalas
for insight
and healing

The mandala as a safe container

The inner dialogue that is continuously present in our minds creates our realities. Unfortunately, for many of us this inner dialogue often takes the form of negative self-talk.

For example, you may not be aware of how much you judge yourself – your appearance, your intelligence, the quality of your work – and project that judgment onto others. When you are not conscious of this habit, you may imagine that others are judging you, rather than being aware of your own harsh attitude toward yourself. It becomes easy to assign the negative voices in your mind to others. Negative self-talk can colour the way you view others and can blind you to their beauty and gifts. It can keep you mired in fear and rob you of the joy and pleasure that are your birthright.

You may be your own worst critic, exaggerating your shortcomings and failing to see your gifts.

When you colour a mandala, you open yourself to self-discovery, healing and creativity.

enables new perspectives to emerge and provides fresh solutions for chronic problems. You may still be aware of the negative thoughts, but they will move to the background. In this way you will be able to see them more objectively and dispassionately.

In a stressful and chaotic world, a mandala functions as a safe container in which you can connect to a part of you that is unchanging, steady and reliable. The simple act of colouring a mandala can help you to relieve stress, make decisions, resolve conflicts with loved ones, work through loss and grief, find relief from addictions and build self-esteem. Colouring mandalas can assist you in discovering your authentic self, which may be hidden under various masks that you have developed in order to please family or friends; it can also help you heal. The rhythmic act of colouring releases you from habitual, narrow thought patterns, enabling you to find creative solutions to problems that you both create and encounter.

Suspending your inner dialogue

By suspending this constant inner talk, and bypassing the negative messages, you can discover an expansive state of authentic awareness and inner knowing. When you are colouring mandalas, your focus is on the colouring, and your inner dialogue is temporarily suspended. When this occurs, you open yourself to self-discovery, healing and creativity. The suspension of negative inner dialogue

Exercise Relax and centre

Colouring mandalas can induce a profound state of relaxation. If you feel frazzled and your nerves are jangled, an hour spent colouring a mandala is the best medicine. The rhythmic motion of colouring will calm your nervous system and soothe your anxious mind.

1 Begin by finding a place where you can be alone and undisturbed. If you have already created a sacred space (see pages 94–95) for colouring mandalas, that's great! If not, add something to the place where you find yourself that symbolizes the peace and contentment you seek – perhaps a religious symbol or something from nature.

2 Gather your colouring materials.

3 Choose a mandala that evokes in you a sense of peace and tranquillity. If you have time, photocopy it onto a larger piece of paper; otherwise, simply colour it in the book using coloured pencils.

4 Before you start to colour, close your eyes and breathe deeply into your abdomen for a few minutes. Most of us breathe in a shallow manner, and this habit is more pronounced when we are tense and worried. Breathing into your abdomen enables your diaphragm to drop down and your lower lungs to fill properly. Getting oxygen to your cells and your brain can do wonders for stress and anxiety. Relax any tense areas of your body, such as your neck or jaw.

5 When you are ready, open your eyes. Begin colouring the mandala you have chosen in any way that feels right to you. Choose colours that feel good to you, and that elicit within you feelings of calm and serenity.

6 When you have completed colouring your mandala, note the colours that you used and consult pages 60–91 for further insight. Then, in your Mandala Journal, make a list of ten ways in which you might bring more relaxation into your life. Choose three suggestions from your list and commit yourself to making those changes within the next month.

Exercise Make a decision

If you have a decision to make, colouring a mandala can help you to find the best way forward. If you are obsessing over your options, or at a loss as to what to do, colouring a mandala will take your mind 'offline' and enable your intuition and deeper knowing to emerge.

1 Choose a mandala that particularly appeals to you from the collection in the Mandala Workbook (see pages 304–85). Do not spend a lot of time on this 'decision' – just pick one that draws your eye.

2 Decide on the materials that you will use to colour it. If you are working in this book, try coloured pencils; if you have enlarged your mandala, you could choose paints, markers or oil pastels.

3 Find a comfortable space where you can be alone, and meditate on your breath for a few minutes, to calm your mind.

4 When you are ready, open your Mandala Journal (see pages 54–55) and write about the decision you would like to make. Let the emotions connected to your decision arise. Perhaps you are afraid that you will make the wrong choice, or you are angry because you would rather not make a decision.

5 Now, begin colouring your mandala. As you do so, allow your thoughts and feelings to come and go. You can think about the decision you have to make, or not – as you wish. It doesn't matter.

6 When you have completed your mandala, take a moment to admire your work. Notice the colours you chose and briefly review the section on colour (see pages 60–91) to help you understand your various colour choices.

7 Now, take a few minutes to write in your Journal about any insights concerning your decision that you may have had as you coloured in your mandala. Notice if your feelings about your impending decision have changed, or if you have a stronger sense of 'knowing' what would be right for you.

Exercise Resolve conflicts with loved ones

If you are having a conflict with your spouse, partner, parent, child or a friend – and you feel you are 'right' and the other person is 'wrong' – then colouring a mandala can help you move beyond polarization toward a creative resolution of your difficulties.

Working with a mandala will give you the space in which to reflect on your situation. It will help you move away from rigid, defensive thinking and become open to your loved one's point of view. This softening and opening to empathy and understanding will enable you to resolve your differences in a way that supports both your own needs and those of your loved one.

1 Sit for a moment with your eyes closed, and call to mind the conflict with your loved one. Breathe into your belly for a few minutes to help yourself feel grounded.

2 Choose a mandala that appeals to you from the collection in the Mandala Workbook (see pages 304–85) and decide on the materials that you will use to colour your mandala. If you wish, enlarge the mandala so that you have access to a broader range of art materials.

3 Now, begin colouring your mandala. As you do so, imagine the conflict from your loved one's point of view. Imagine how he or she feels and thinks about the issue at hand. Try to generate compassion for yourself and your loved one simultaneously. Resolving a conflict is not about winning an argument, but about finding a way to accommodate each person's needs.

4 When you have completed your mandala, write in your Mandala Journal about your insights. Sometimes, just acknowledging your loved one's point of view can shift the energy between you. Share any realizations you may have with him or her to help you resolve your differences.

Exercise Let go of addictions

The word 'addiction' may call to mind alcohol or substance abuse, and you may suffer from either or both. But there are other, often unrecognized addictions. For example, you may be addicted to certain foods, such as ice cream or sweets, which in excess can harm your health. You may have an addiction to the Internet, causing you to neglect your relationships and your work. Or you may be addicted to sex or pornography. Any compulsive activity can be an addiction. This exercise will help you heal from your addictions, whatever they may be.

1 Find a place where you can be alone and free of distractions. Sit quietly for a few minutes and breathe deeply to relax. When you are ready, write in your Mandala Journal about the ways in which your addiction is harming you and your loved ones.

2 Choose a mandala that speaks to you from the collection in the Mandala Workbook (see pages 304–85) and decide on the materials you will use to colour it.

3 When you are ready, begin colouring the mandala. As you do so, acknowledge your addiction, but also generate a feeling of love and compassion for yourself. Love is the wish for happiness; compassion is the desire to be free of suffering.

4 As you colour, reflect on the source of your addiction. What pain or injury are you trying to anaesthetize? Perhaps you were a victim of abuse during your childhood, or you have a range of fears that you are afraid to face.

5 When you have completed your mandala, acknowledge your courage in facing this difficult problem. Take a few minutes to write in your journal about any insights you may have discovered concerning your addiction. In addition, write down one thing you could do to overcome this addiction. For example, you could commit to reading a self-help book about your addiction, joining a support group or seeing a counsellor.

Exercise Work through grief

Life is impermanent, and grief is a reaction to the inevitable losses we will face during our lifetimes. We grieve over the death of our loved ones. But grief can manifest itself for any loss – for example, when we divorce, lose a job, a lover, a friend or a pet. Women often grieve when they miscarry. We can grieve in response to diagnosis of serious illness.

It is never inappropriate to grieve, because loss is part of our human condition. If we allow ourselves to acknowledge and feel our loss and sadness, then our pain will lessen over time as we move on to embrace our present life.

1 Find a place where you can be alone and free of distractions. Sit quietly for a few minutes and breathe deeply to relax and calm yourself. When you are ready, write in your Mandala Journal about the loss you are feeling. Your grief may be over the death of a loved one or the loss of a treasured object. It is okay to feel what you are feeling.

2 Choose an appropriate mandala from the collection in the Mandala Workbook (see pages 304–85) and decide on the materials you will use to colour it.

3 When you are ready, begin colouring your mandala. As you do so, bring to mind the loss for which you are grieving. Allow your feelings and thoughts to come and go as you colour each part of the mandala.

4 Notice your colour choices, and the beauty of the mandala as it emerges as a result of your effort. Out of your grief and loss you are giving birth to a work of art.

5 When you have completed your mandala, acknowledge your bravery in facing your grief and loss. Take a few minutes to write in your Journal about your feelings and insights.

Exercise Heal from illness

Mandalas are powerful healing tools. Colouring mandalas can boost your immune system, reduce stress, combat depression, reduce pain, lower blood pressure and stimulate the release of melatonin – a hormone that can slow ageing and promote good sleep. If you are suffering from an illness, colouring mandalas can make it easier for your body to heal.

Mandalas are so effective that they have entered mainstream medicine. In the US the University of California at Irvine Cancer Centre and the University of Pennsylvania Cancer Centre offer mandala workshops to cancer survivors.

1 Find a place where you can be alone and free of distractions. Sit quietly for a few minutes and breathe deeply to relax and calm yourself. When you are ready, write in your Mandala Journal about your illness and your desire to heal. Compose a paragraph or two describing yourself as if you were totally healed.

2 Choose a mandala that suggests healing to you from the collection in the Mandala Workbook (see pages 304–85) and decide on the materials you will use to colour it.

3 When you are ready, begin colouring the mandala. As you do so, acknowledge your illness, but also focus on the truth of impermanence and on the tremendous ability of the body to heal.

4 Continue colouring and, as you colour, express gratitude for all the people that are helping you in your illness. Include family members, friends, neighbours, doctors, nurses, alternative-medicine practitioners, counsellors and even clergy. Feel them surrounding you with loving, healing energy.

5 When you have completed your mandala, notice the colours you chose. Consult the section on colour (see pages 60–91) for further insight. Hang up your mandala where you can see it every day. Let it remind you of the wisdom of the body and the healing power of the universe.

Exercise Manifest your desires

If you want to manifest your desires, you must first be fully present
in the moment. Colouring mandalas will help you stay present and
focused. When you manifest a desire, it has to be something that you
want for yourself. Trying to make someone else be or do something for
you is an act of aggression. Be specific about what it is you want to buy
or have. For example, focus on having a new car or paying off your
debts. Finally, and most importantly, make sure that what you want is
something that is in your best interests and for the highest good of all.

1 Find a place where you can be alone and
free of distractions. Sit quietly for a few
minutes and breathe deeply to relax and
calm yourself. When you are ready, write in
your Mandala Journal about what it is you
wish to manifest. Be as clear as possible,
and write about *why* you want it and desire
it. Determine whether it is in your best
interest and for the highest good of all.

2 Choose a mandala from the collection in
the Mandala Workbook (see pages 304–85)
and decide on the materials that you will
use to colour it.

3 Begin colouring your mandala. As you do
so, visualize what it is that you desire in
detail. See and feel yourself having it.

4 As you colour, notice any resistance,
guilt or sense of unworthiness. Let yourself
know that you are worthy of attaining any
dream, vision or goal that you desire. If
you feel any need for love, acceptance
or permission from others before you
have what you desire, then replace those
feelings with self-love.

5 When you have completed your mandala,
hang it in a place where you can see it every
day. When you view your mandala, visualize
what it is that you would like to manifest.

Exercise Discover your true calling

The word 'vocation' comes from the Latin word *vocare*, which means 'to call'. Whether you are young, middle-aged or nearing retirement, it is never too late to discover your true calling. It is normal to take many years before pursuing or discovering your vocation. The important thing is to pursue it and not get sidetracked by an uninspiring but well-paid job, or by trying to live out a parent's dream. Colouring mandalas can help you explore your calling – work that best suits your authentic self.

1 Find a place where you can be alone and free of distractions. Sit quietly for a few minutes and breathe deeply to relax.

2 Choose a mandala from the collection in the Mandala Workbook (see pages 304–85) and decide on the materials that you will use to colour your mandala.

3 Fear of exploring your true calling can keep you from knowing what it is. For example, you may be afraid of ending up poor. Let these worst-case scenarios emerge, then politely ask them to get out of the way. As you begin to colour, invite the truth into your life so that you can begin to pursue your dreams.

4 You may find it hard to imagine doing what you love as a profession. As you

colour, open yourself to ways of bridging the two worlds of your passion and making a living. Know that life will evolve naturally, if you listen to your inner self and pursue what you truly enjoy.

5 Real knowing comes from experience, rather than intellectual activity. If you have no idea where to start, as you colour your mandala, let insights emerge from the experiences you have already had in the world of work. You already know a lot about what makes you deeply happy and what does not.

6 When you have finished your mandala, write in your Mandala Journal what you have discovered about your true calling.

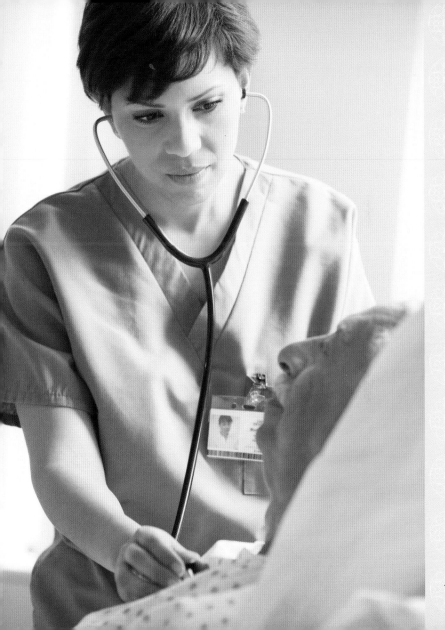

Exercise Build your self-esteem

How well do you respect yourself? Do you honour and appreciate yourself every day? Or do you put yourself down at every turn, contributing to your sense of low self-worth or self-esteem? How does this negative attitude toward yourself affect your behaviour? When you suffer from low self-esteem, you may do things that are harmful to yourself. For example, you may be overeating and neglecting your health. Or you may be undermining yourself by showing up late for work.

1 Find a place where you can be alone and free of distractions. Sit quietly for a few minutes and breathe deeply. When you are ready, write in your Mandala Journal about how you feel about yourself. If you suffer from low self-esteem, acknowledging this is essential. Only then can you address your lack of self-love and self-regard.

2 Choose a mandala from the collection in the Mandala Workbook (see pages 304–85) and decide on the materials that you will use to colour it.

3 When you are ready, begin colouring your mandala. As you do so, generate a sense of love and compassion for yourself. Tell yourself that you are worthy of love and compassion just as you are.

4 Continuing colouring and, as you colour, think of three positive qualities that you possess. For example, you may be a good parent or a good listener or a good cook. Think about how you manifest those qualities and how you use them to help yourself and those around you.

5 When you have completed your mandala, write down on it your three positive qualities. When you view your mandala, let it remind you that your life has tremendous value and that you have many gifts to share with the world.

Exercise Relieve your depression

If you suffer from depression, you may be a perfectionist. Demanding too much of yourself, and then failing to measure up to your unrealistic expectations, can lead to bouts of self-hatred and depression. Colouring mandalas induces a deep sense of calm and well-being – a great antidote to the negative thinking that accompanies depression. For an hour or so, you can give yourself permission to relax.

The beauty of this exercise is that colouring doesn't require perfection. There is no way to make a mistake when you are colouring a mandala. The nurturing circular form of the mandala functions as a container to hold you until you can return to balance and wholeness.

1 Choose a time when you can be alone in a relaxing and comfortable space. Sit quietly for a few minutes and breathe deeply to relax and calm yourself. When you are ready, write in your Mandala Journal about your depression. Describe how you feel and note any negative attitudes toward yourself, especially a feeling that you have 'failed' in some way.

2 Choose a mandala from the collection in the Mandala Workbook (see pages 304–85)

and decide on the materials that you will use to colour your mandala. If you wish, light a candle or two.

3 Play music in the background or listen on your headphones. Choose music that is soothing to your ear. As you colour your mandala, remember to breathe deeply into your belly. In this exercise you are giving your mind and body a well-needed rest. Simply listen to beautiful music and colour the mandala. There is no right or wrong way to colour it; there are no right or wrong colours. The act of colouring – in and of itself – is healing.

4 When you have completed your mandala, make a list of ten of your most positive aspects and note how colouring this mandala while listening to music made you feel.

Exercise Quit smoking

Smoking is a very difficult addiction to break. Experts say that quitting this habit can be as difficult as giving up heroin. So congratulations if you have decided to stop smoking – you are a brave person. It is possible that you will have significant withdrawal symptoms, accompanied by feelings of irritability and anxiety.

Try getting a prescription from your doctor for a smoking-cessation aid, or attending a support group to help you through the toughest part. Colouring mandalas can be another tool in your arsenal to help calm your nerves as you give up your smoking habit. Holding a pencil and colouring is a great substitute activity when you are tempted to pick up a cigarette.

When you colour mandalas as an aid to quitting smoking, it is best to colour them in this book. It is small enough that you can carry it around your house with you or out in your garden, along with a set of coloured pencils. You can even take this book and your coloured pencils to work, to use during your break or at lunch.

When you colour mandalas to help you quit smoking, feel free to watch television, talk to family members, sit on a bus or talk on the phone at the same time. The idea is to have something constructive and healing to do when you want to smoke and the withdrawal symptoms are getting the better of you.

As you colour your mandala, simply enjoy the rhythmic activity of colouring and the beauty of the form as it emerges. The aim is to keep your hand moving and occupied. Substituting your desire to hold a cigarette with the activity of colouring with a pencil will help you give up the habits and rituals of smoking, such as a cigarette after a meal, which act as powerful triggers for the desire to smoke.

Exercise Lose weight

Sorry to disappoint, but colouring mandalas will not make you thinner. Weight loss requires a combination of eating healthy foods and daily exercise. What colouring mandalas can do is provide emotional support.

Obesity is on the rise in most of the industrialized world, as grocery stores and restaurants are flooded with foods that contain highly addictive combinations of sugar, salt and fats. In other words, the deck is stacked against you. It takes effort to wean yourself off addictive fast-food hamburgers and sugary desserts and switch to wholegrains, legumes, fresh vegetables and fruit, and high-quality, lean protein. Colouring mandalas can help you stay calm and focused as you make this difficult but life-changing transition to a healthy diet and weight.

1 Choose a time late in the day when you can be alone. Sit quietly for a few minutes and breathe deeply to relax and calm yourself. When you are ready, record in your Mandala Journal what you weigh, what you ate today, if you exercised and how much. Describe how you feel emotionally, and note if you have adhered to your new eating plan and exercise regime. Refrain from judging yourself.

2 Select a mandala from the collection in the Mandala Workbook (see pages 304–85) and decide on the materials that you will use to colour it.

3 As you colour your mandala, remember first to breathe deeply into your belly, then feel yourself inhabiting your entire body from your toes to the tip of your head. If you had a good day with your efforts at weight loss, congratulate yourself. If you had a bad day, gained weight or ate unhealthy foods, let it go. Generate a feeling of love for yourself just as you are today. Resolve to take better care of yourself tomorrow.

4 When you have finished colouring your mandala, write an encouraging message to yourself with a pen in the margin.

Exercise Get through a divorce

For some, divorce is mutually desired and the marriage is dissolved without acrimony. But most divorces are difficult, painful, even devastating experiences. Even if the marriage has been going badly, ending it may feel traumatic, especially if you are the one left for another person. And then, if there are young children involved, you will have to continue a working relationship in order to care for your children. Colouring mandalas can help you work through your emotions.

1 Choose a time when you can be alone. Sit quietly for a few minutes and breathe deeply to relax and calm yourself. When you are ready, record in your Mandala Journal the current feelings you have about your divorce. It doesn't matter if your divorce is under way, very recent or decades old. A divorce is not an event, but rather a process.

2 Choose a mandala from the collection in the Mandala Workbook (see pages 304–85) and decide on the materials that you will use to colour it.

3 As you colour your mandala, pay attention to your emotions about the loss of your relationship, rather than to your thoughts. If you are sad, let that emerge.

If you are angry, it is okay to admit that you are. Perhaps you are afraid of the future and fearful you won't find another partner. Rather than getting lost in angry imaginary conversations, just let the feelings flow as you colour. Notice if they evolve as you colour your mandala.

4 When you have finished colouring it, close your eyes and breathe deeply for a few minutes. Focus on your breath rather than your thoughts and emotions. Imagine that your thoughts and emotions are like storm clouds, passing by overhead and disappearing into the distance.

Exercise Contemplate generosity

What exactly is generosity? The Buddha described three kinds of generosity. The first is giving material goods, such as money, food or clothing. The second is giving comfort to those who are afraid. For example, if a friend is diagnosed with a serious disease, you do what you can to ease their fears and help them cope. The third is the act of mentoring, and the sharing of spiritual knowledge and wisdom.

1 Choose a mandala that you would like to colour from the Mandala Workbook (see pages 304–85) and find a place where you can be alone and undisturbed. Take a moment to sit quietly and centre yourself.

2 Begin at the outer edge of your mandala and work inward. As you begin colouring, think about your attitudes to giving. Do you find giving stressful, or a financial drain? Do you love opportunities to give others gifts, such as birthdays or holidays? As you colour, consider where in that spectrum you fall.

3 Continue colouring and let any pain about past gift-giving emerge. Maybe your gift to someone was rejected, or you felt shame because you did not have money to give gifts. Also consider any joyful memories of gift-giving.

4 Moving inward, think about what you have to give others, other than material or monetary gifts. Simply listening to a friend can be a gift. Relieving fear is a form of generosity. The giving of your time and companionship is more valuable than a material gift.

5 Now, as you approach the centre of your mandala, consider your knowledge and wisdom. Is there a young person in your life who needs mentoring? Alternatively, is there a group or organization that could use your expertise? Are you willing to give away your knowledge and wisdom?

6 When you have completed your mandala, write in your Mandala Journal about how generosity plays a part in your life.

Exercise Integrate your life

Modern life demands that you play many roles – parent, friend, spouse, partner, sibling, church member, aunt, professional. As a result, you may feel fragmented and split, because your energies are pulled in many directions. You may feel you are a different person in different situations rather than one whole, integrated human being. The mandala can help bring all the 'parts' of your life together and anchor you in your authentic self. You may wear many different hats, but working with mandalas can help you integrate your roles and your different personal qualities.

1 Choose a mandala with a complex design from the Mandala Workbook (see pages 304–85). Find a place where you can be alone and undisturbed.

2 In your Mandala Journal write down a list of the many roles you play in life: for example, spouse, parent, sibling, employee, teacher, mentor or friend. Then list your qualities, both positive and negative: for instance, creative, selfish, efficient, emotional, loving, loyal and impatient.

3 Now begin colouring anywhere you like on the mandala, using as many different colours, shades and techniques as you desire. Refer to your lists as you colour. Mentally place the different roles and

aspects of yourself wherever you like on your mandala, and then colour them with shades that you feel are appropriate.

4 As you colour, notice how your separate personas and qualities are merging into one beautiful design.

5 When you have completed your mandala, take a moment to reflect on your various roles and qualities. Notice that they are now part of a coherent pattern and are held in the beauty of the mandala.

6 Consult the section on colour (see pages 60–91) to gain insights into the colours you have used. Finish by writing in your journal about how to better integrate your life.

Exercise Inhabit your body

Most of us live from the neck up. From time to time we may 'feel' our bodies when attention to movement or posture is required. For example, in a yoga class we pay attention to our form and balance. But actually inhabiting the body is a different thing. Most indigenous peoples have full awareness of their bodies and, simultaneously, of the world around them. But in modern urban cultures we put much greater emphasis on mental activity, and lose touch with our bodies and surroundings.

1 First, choose a mandala to colour from the Mandala Workbook (see pages 304–85). Then find a time and place where you can be alone and undisturbed.

2 Take a few minutes to breathe into your belly. Exhale slowly and repeat.

3 Now start to colour your mandala. As you do so, begin by breathing into your feet. Try to maintain awareness of your feet and, simultaneously, of the sensation of colouring. You may feel as if you are alternating at first, but try to maintain awareness of your mandala and your feet at the same time.

4 As you continue colouring, bring your awareness to your legs, then your knees and the rest of your body, part by part. Breathe into each part of your body as you colour. Try to maintain awareness of the parts that you have already worked with as you move to new areas of your body. Simultaneously, maintain awareness of the mandala and of the sensation of colouring.

5 When you have finished colouring, meditate for a few minutes on the sensation of fully inhabiting your body while you enjoy your completed mandala. Try to bring this awareness into your daily life on a regular basis.

Exercise Forgive yourself and others

Forgiveness is a process that you enter into when you choose to heal. It does not deny, minimize or justify what others have done to you, or the pain that you have suffered. Nor does it minimize or justify what you have done to others – or yourself. Forgiveness encourages you to realize that the events that triggered those feelings are in the past. Because you are keeping the old hurts and shame alive, you are damaging yourself. Forgiveness brings with it feelings of wellness and freedom.

1 First, choose a mandala to colour from the Mandala Workbook (see pages 304–85). Then find a time and place where you can be alone and undisturbed.

2 Now, as you begin to colour, imagine yourself letting go of your resentment and anger over past hurts, as if you were dropping a very heavy bag. As you move through each section of the mandala, imagine your burden of anger and resentment getting lighter. Contemplate that you no longer need your anger and resentment as a weapon to punish others, or as a shield to protect yourself by keeping others away.

3 As you continue to colour, consider that the person who hurt you is the same as you,

in that he or she wants to be happy and avoid suffering. Mentally let go of your identity as a victim and embrace yourself as an artist. Note how hiding yourself in your anger has prevented you from joy and healing.

4 If you can, generate a feeling of compassion for the person who harmed you. If you have shame from your own past behaviour, generate a sense of love and compassion for yourself.

5 When you have completed your mandala, write a letter in your Mandala Journal to the person who harmed you, forgiving them for having hurt you. Then write a letter forgiving yourself for anything that causes you shame.

Exercise Contemplate impermanence

You and everything else in the universe are in a continual state of transformation. If you recognize that all things and experiences, people and relationships are impermanent, you can relax with their coming and going. Seeing that change is inevitable helps you to let go of clinging to the way things are or of resisting how they will inevitably change.

1 Choose a mandala that you would like to colour from the Mandala Workbook (see pages 304–85).

2 As you begin to colour, recognize that one day your life will come to an end. Recognizing impermanence – especially your own – can help you look closely at your priorities and values. Opening to the ordinary level of impermanence in a deep and profound way can bring tremendous wisdom. Think about what is most important to you, and whether you are living your life in alignment with your highest values and priorities.

3 Pay attention to the moment-to-moment arising and passing of every perceivable experience. Notice your mandala changing before your eyes. Contemplate on the fact that everything is constantly in flux – even experiences and things that ordinarily seem fixed and solid.

4 As you fill your mandala with colour, consider that it is impossible to cling to a moment or an experience, because everything simply flashes in and out of existence.

5 Now contemplate the ideas and concepts that you cling to. Are you defensive and rigid when it comes to politics, religion or your ideas about how to do something 'the right way'? One of our most ingrained attachments is to self, self-image and self-identity.

6 When you have completed your mandala, record in your Mandala Journal your insights about impermanence.

Exercise Practise perseverance

Perseverance is the antidote to procrastination – the all-too-human habit of avoiding a task because of fear or anger. Avoidance of work is often bound up with anger at having been asked to do something, with fear of judgment or with a lack of the necessary skills to do the task. Perseverance is the quality necessary to break through old patterns of avoidance; it is a conscious decision to bring joyful effort to whatever you do. Breaking the procrastination habit requires introspection to understand the issues underlying the behaviour, and dedicated effort to overcome what is holding you back.

1 Choose a mandala to colour from the Mandala Workbook (see pages 304–85) and find a space where you can be alone and undisturbed. Take a moment to relax and centre yourself.

2 As you begin colouring your mandala, call to mind times when procrastination caused you difficulties. It could be that procrastination made your work suffer or even lost you your job; it may have cost you money or a relationship.

3 Continue colouring and ask yourself what lies behind your procrastination. If you are afraid, try to identify the fear. Perhaps you are afraid of mediocrity, or that

you do not really know how to do the task at hand. With knowledge comes the power to solve your issues concerning avoidance.

4 Now imagine forging ahead on a project that frightened you in the past. Visualize yourself working steadily and happily and completing the project on time. Mentally congratulate yourself for having the courage to face your fear.

5 When you have completed your mandala (and it is important to complete this one), write in your Mandala Journal about any insights you have gained concerning your problem with procrastination and its antidote – perseverance.

Exercise Practise patience

Patience is an antidote to anger. Patience gives you breathing space, and time to sort out what lies behind your anger. Anger is often based on projection. For example, an office mate's shoddy work infuriates you when you know, deep down, that your work is lacking as well. When you take the time to colour a mandala and meditate on your anger, you can review it with more honesty and objectivity. When it comes to aggression or injustice, patience helps you develop an inner calmness and insight to deal with these situations in an effective way.

1 Choose a mandala to colour from the Mandala Workbook (see pages 304–85), and find a space where you can be alone and undisturbed. Relax and centre yourself.

2 As you begin colouring your mandala, call to mind a person or situation that has evoked your anger. Ask yourself if you are guilty of the same behaviour or attitude. Have you done this same thing to others?

3 Continuing colouring and consider whether you are exaggerating the negative aspects of this person and forgetting that he or she also has good qualities.

4 As you fill in your mandala, ask yourself what lies behind your anger. For example,

are you hurt? Are you afraid? If you are afraid or hurt, try to be specific about your pain or fear.

5 Notice how, when a strong thought of anger arises, it overwhelms you and destroys your peace and presence of mind, but with contemplation, and through the physical movements of colouring, your anger subsides.

6 When you have completed your mandala, write in your Mandala Journal about any insights that you have gained concerning your anger. Depending on what you have discovered, either decide to talk to the person or use the knowledge you have gained in future situations.

Exercise Practise mindfulness

Mindfulness is a practice based on the understanding that the present is the only time you really have. How do you practise mindfulness? By choosing to pay attention, in the present moment, to your physical sensations, perceptions, emotions, thoughts and mental imagery. You observe without judgment what is going on with you right now, in this moment. When you mindfully participate in life, you replace habitual reactions with more accurate perceptions of what is going on, both externally and internally.

1 Choose a mandala to colour from the Mandala Workbook (see pages 304–85). Then settle yourself in a place where you can colour undisturbed.

2 Before you begin, take a moment to notice where you are sitting. Note the colour of the walls, and of the furniture and the floor. Listen to any sounds in the room, however faint. Perhaps a bird is singing outside, or a car is going by in the distance. Pay attention to the quality of the light in the room.

3 As you start colouring, pay attention to your body and how it feels. Are you comfortable where you are sitting? Do you have any pain anywhere? Breathe into each

part of your body. Choose segments of your mandala to represent different parts of your body and then practise body-awareness as you colour them.

4 Next, pay attention to your hand as it moves across your mandala. How does it feel? Notice the paper the mandala is printed on. Let any thoughts come and go.

5 As you colour, simply be in the present moment. Let the colours choose themselves as you slowly fill in your mandala.

6 When it is complete, be mindful of how the various colours affect you. Simply pay attention to how you feel and what you are thinking in this moment.

Exercise Practise gratitude

A person who experiences gratitude is often able to cope more effectively with everyday stress, recover more quickly from illness and enjoy a greater sense of well-being. Gratitude is one of the few things that can change your life quickly and in a measurable way. When stressful things happen, such as job loss or diagnosis of an illness, it is easy to think negatively. But practising gratitude can help you shift from self-defeating thoughts into a broader, more balanced view. In trying times, gratitude helps you focus on what is working in your life and how you can cope with what has happened. Gratitude brings you into the present and balances the negative with the positive.

1 Choose a mandala with a fairly complex design from the Mandala Workbook (see pages 304–85).

2 In this exercise you are going to colour each segment of the mandala to represent something for which you feel grateful. These things, or people, or experiences, can be large or small, significant or seemingly insignificant. For example, you may feel grateful for your spouse, or for the prompt delivery of your mail today. If your mandala has a lot of segments to colour, you may feel that you will run out of things to be grateful for. But this will not happen, which is a revelation in itself.

3 Begin colouring the first segment of your mandala. Start with something you normally take for granted. For example, the cup of tea you had at breakfast, or the bird singing outside your window. Express gratitude that you have tea that you like, a mug, a source of clean water and a way to heat it. As you move from one segment to the next, express gratitude for each and every thing that you can think of.

Exercise Review your life

From time to time it is useful to review your life as it has unfolded from your birth until the present. You can do this by looking at each year, or you can consider five-year increments. Probably you will find a story of difficulties and accomplishments, joys and sorrows, important influences and people, and both painful and joyful relationships. By reviewing your life you have a chance to see repeating patterns and issues. You may find difficulties with your work life or relationships that you want to examine and change, as well as strength and courage you did not know you had.

1 Choose a mandala to colour from the Mandala Workbook (see pages 304–85) and then close your eyes. Bring to mind your earliest years.

2 Begin colouring your mandala in the centre and work outward. Recall any family stories of your birth as you fill in the centre. Then, moving outward, bring to mind your early childhood years. Visualize your city or town, your bedroom and your house. Think about your first school and your teachers.

3 Bring to mind your teen years. Let any good or bad memories emerge, without censoring them. When you are ready, move on to your young adult years, and your later years up until the present.

4 As you colour your mandala, think about your significant relationships – with your parents, siblings and other family members, your teachers and mentors, your minister or priest, and your close friends and love interests. Recall any life-changing events, such as a marriage, an important job or an illness.

5 When you have completed your mandala, review the meaning of the colours you have chosen (see pages 60–91). Then write about your life review in your Mandala Journal, touching on where you have been, what you have accomplished and what you would like your future to be.

Exercise See the colours in nature

No one needs to be told that the colours of nature are staggeringly beautiful. But it takes time and attention to see them and appreciate them. In this exercise you will be asked to find a place outdoors where you can sit relatively undisturbed. Then you will colour a mandala using the colours in nature that you observe around you. You can choose one flower, an entire forest or a stream or other body of water. The longer you look at nature, the more colours you will see. What you thought was a brown leaf may have 20 different colours on its surface.

1 Choose a mandala that you would like to colour from the Mandala Workbook (see pages 304–85) and select a place outdoors where you can sit undisturbed. Bring a folding chair or a blanket, your coloured pencils and your Mandala Journal.

2 Take a moment to really look at the scene, or natural object, that you would like to capture in your mandala. Then begin to colour, following the colours you see in front of you.

3 Don't worry if the colours aren't exact. Do the best you can with the art supplies you have. More importantly, let your feelings about the natural world around you inform your colouring. Connect to

nature through your body and your eyes as you bring the hues around you, and in front of you, into your mandala.

4 As you colour, notice whether more and more colours reveal themselves to you, the longer you look. Try not to think about colour or nature – just relax and make the connection with your hand, your eyes and your body.

5 When your mandala is complete, sit for a few minutes and enjoy it and the nature around you. Then write in your Mandala Journal about your experience.

Exercise Manage a financial crisis

A financial crisis can be stressful and frightening. Losing your savings on the stock market, losing your income, finding yourself unable to manage your credit-card debt or pay your rent or mortgage can be terrifying experiences. In the short term you can find less expensive living arrangements, and generally cut back on expenses. In the longer term you can look for a better job and pay off your debt. Colouring mandalas will help support you as you explore and resolve your financial crisis.

1 Find a place where you can be alone and free of distractions. Sit quietly for a few minutes and breathe deeply.

2 Choose a mandala that appeals to you from the collection in the Mandala Workbook (see pages 304–85) and decide what materials you will use to colour it.

3 When you are ready, begin colouring your mandala. Start from the centre and work outward. As you colour the centre, acknowledge your financial crisis and express any feelings you have about it. For example, you may feel frightened, angry or helpless.

4 As you move outward from the centre, begin imagining ways in which you can

solve your financial problem. Just let the ideas flow – don't censor any of them.

5 Note any feelings of shame or guilt that arise. If you caused your problems through irresponsibility or negligence – perhaps overspending on your credit cards, or buying a house beyond your means – acknowledge what you did and forgive yourself. You can start to turn your life around this moment.

6 When you have completed your mandala, write in your Mandala Journal any insights you gained that may help you to resolve your financial crisis.

Exercise Survive a job loss

Whether you were laid off, made redundant for budgetary reasons or fired for a cause, losing your job can be devastating to your self-esteem. At first you may be in shock as you experience a rollercoaster of feelings – anger, sadness, regret, shame. Your work may be a big part of your identity and your closest friends may be your workmates. And losing your income can be as stressful as losing your identity and your friends.

Colouring mandalas can help you sort through your feelings and find gainful employment once again. In some cases, losing a job opens you up to a much better situation than you had before or even knew was possible.

1 Find a place where you can be alone and free of distractions. Sit quietly for a few minutes and breathe deeply.

2 Choose a mandala that appeals to you from the collection in the Mandala Workbook (see pages 304–85) and decide what materials you will use to colour it.

3 When you are ready, begin colouring your mandala in any way you like. As you do so, acknowledge any feelings you have about losing your job and daily contact with your workmates. It is okay if you experience anger or feel like crying.

4 When you are halfway through colouring your mandala, begin to imagine your ideal job. Visualize what your day is like, what you are doing and where you are working. Perhaps you are working for yourself in a new business. Imagine the people you see everyday, either new workmates or clients. Perhaps you opened a bakery or a coffee house in your neighbourhood, or turned your weekend tinkering with cars into a full service garage. Let your imagination run free.

5 When you have completed your mandala, write in your Mandala Journal about how you feel about losing your job, and any insights you may have gained about which direction your future should take.

Exercise Discover your authentic self

The world bombards us with messages about what to do, how to be, what to think and what to wear. These messages come from family, church, schools and friends. Advertising tells us what we should feel and want. But who are you really? And what do you actually think and feel? What is it that you really want from life?

1 Find a place where you can be alone and free of distractions. Sit quietly for a few minutes and breathe deeply to relax and calm yourself.

2 Choose a mandala that appeals to your aesthetic sense from the collection in the Mandala Workbook (see pages 304–85) and decide on the materials that you will use to colour it.

3 When you are ready, begin colouring your mandala. This time start from the outer edges and work toward the centre.

4 As you move closer to the centre, let yourself be more and more who you really are. For example, you may be a lawyer, but inside you are a professional artist. Or you may have a desk job, but long to work with your hands. Or you may be pretending to yourself and your friends to be straight, but know deep inside that you are gay. Sometimes it is very difficult to be your authentic self. This is not an exercise in self-judgment, but one in self-love.

5 When you reach the centre, close your eyes and experience yourself as you really are. Know that your authentic self is not an identity set in stone, but a way of living that is congruent with your deepest needs and values at that moment.

6 When you have completed your mandala, take a few minutes to write in your Mandala Journal about your feelings and insights.

Exercise Celebrate your birthday

Birthday celebrations usually involve your friends and loved ones. You may receive gifts, be taken out to dinner, be the honoured guest at a party and, of course, have a special cake made for you. If your cake has candles, you may be invited to make a wish for the coming year. But there is another way to celebrate a birthday, and that is to take some time alone to reflect on where you are at this point in your life. Colouring a birthday mandala can be that special gift to yourself.

1 Find a place where you can be alone and free of distractions. Take as long as you want to write in your Mandala Journal about your birthday. Express how you feel about this particular birthday – you may feel a whole range of emotions that are contradictory.

2 Choose a mandala that resonates with how you feel at this moment. As you begin colouring, think back over the past year and recall your accomplishments, no matter how small or seemingly insignificant they seem. Congratulate yourself on what you have accomplished.

3 Continue colouring, and recall the difficulties you encountered in the past year and what you did to resolve them. Congratulate yourself on your hard work

since your last birthday – in supporting yourself, taking care of others and trying to live a good life. Resist any tendency to dwell on the negative. Your birthday is a time for celebration.

4 Now bring to mind what you would like to manifest in the coming year. Perhaps you would like to be healthier by your next birthday, or to have a new job that makes you want to get out of bed in the morning, or to have met your soulmate. Visualize what you would like the next year to be.

5 When you have completed your mandala, either frame it or store it in a place where you can refer to it often.

Exercise Survive the holidays

Wherever you live in the world, you probably have special holidays that you spend with family and friends. Holidays are meant to be joyful celebrations, and usually they are. But you are not alone if you also find them stressful. If you are preparing the holiday meal, you may feel pressure to get everything just right. If you are exchanging gifts, you may feel pressure to find the appropriate item for each person. Taking time to colour a mandala can help you relax, survive and enjoy your holidays.

1 Find a place where you can be alone and away from your family. Sit still and follow your breath for a few minutes to calm and centre yourself.

2 Choose a mandala from the Mandala Workbook (see pages 304–85) that feels right for the holiday you are celebrating. As you begin colouring, think about the meaning of the holiday. If it is religious, such as Christmas or Chanukkah, take a moment to reflect on what this means for you. If it is a secular holiday, such as New Year or Boxing Day, think about its origins and what meaning or associations it has for you.

3 If you are having any discomfort on this holiday, explore why that is. If you are feeling angry with someone in your family, acknowledge your anger and then imagine you are that family member. Try to feel what he or she is feeling.

4 If you are experiencing stress or tension around this holiday, breathe slowly and deeply as you colour. The act of colouring will help relieve your stress. Don't deny that the stress is there, but try to focus on the positive and joyful aspects of this day. Think of three things about this holiday that you enjoy.

5 When you have finished colouring your mandala, close your eyes once again and breathe deeply for five minutes.

Exercise Explore your outer, inner and secret selves

Your outer self is the self you present to the world. It is your persona – the face you want others to see and the qualities you want others to admire, such as your ability to conduct a business meeting. Your inner self is the person you really are – your authentic self. You let those who are close to you see this inner self. Your secret self is hardly ever revealed to anyone, and sometimes you may not even know who he or she is.

1 Choose a mandala from the Mandala Workbook (see pages 304–85) that has a defined centre, inner ring and outer area.

2 Begin colouring the outer area of the mandala, which represents the face you show to the world and your social self, or public persona.

3 Continue colouring and move toward the inner ring, which represents what you consider to be your deeper nature, or 'who you really are'. You may let your friends and loved ones see this deeper, more vulnerable side of yourself.

4 Finally you will arrive at the centre, which represents your secret, most private self. This self you rarely, if ever, share with anyone, and it may be something of a mystery to you as well. Your most secret self can be a source of hidden treasure. It can hold talents and gifts waiting to be developed, or love and compassion waiting to be expressed toward yourself and others. It may also hold old wounds from your past, waiting to be addressed and healed.

5 When you have completed your mandala, meditate on these three aspects of yourself, then write in your Mandala Journal about your experience and insights.

Mandalas in spiritual traditions

Mandala meditations to deepen your spiritual understanding

In the previous exercises you coloured Hindu, Buddhist, Christian, Celtic and Native American mandalas. These mandalas are beautiful to behold, and colouring them can be a rewarding and healing experience.

Beyond this, these ancient mandalas symbolize a complex set of spiritual beliefs unique to each culture. In some of these traditions mandalas still function as an aid to meditation and as a blueprint or guide for spiritual growth.

Hindus and Buddhists continue to use mandalas for solitary meditation, and within different rituals and ceremonies. Native Americans use sand paintings in healing rituals. The Christian mandala – the rose window – contains known symbols and images, and although there is no meditation associated with them, they can still be used today as an aid to meditation. Celtic mandalas do not have specific teachings or meditations associated with them, but are thought to represent the principles of the pagan and Celtic traditions.

Mandalas in different traditions

In this section you are invited to colour specific mandalas from the Hindu, Buddhist, Christian, Celtic and Native American traditions. As you colour each part of the mandala, you will be introduced to its spiritual meaning.

Hindu and Buddhist mandalas are two-dimensional representations of a three-dimensional spiritual world. Mandalas may appear to be flat, but they represent the multi-dimensional abode of a Buddhist or Hindu deity who functions as an archetype of enlightenment. The mandala is filled with symbols that represent many layers of meaning. Unpacking and comprehending each symbol helps the meditator to achieve deeper layers of understanding and to experience more subtle states of consciousness.

In the Christian mandala the temporal and spiritual worlds are combined. The ordinary world is represented on the periphery or bottom half of the rose window, and Heaven is represented in the upper half or the centre, where Mary, Christ, God or the Holy Spirit resides.

In the Native American tradition, in ancient times tribes constructed large

Native American medicine wheels are used for astronomical, ritual, healing, and teaching purposes.

mandalas called 'medicine wheels' in the landscape, using stones and other markers. Many of these ancient medicine wheels can be found today in the Great Plains of the United States and in parts of Canada.

Hindu mandalas

The essence of Hindu tantric thought is that all existence is governed by a supreme consciousness, an infinite reservoir of collective energy from which everything emerges and into which everything returns.

In the Hindu worldview there is unity in all creation. The centre of all existence is the 'One', or the 'Cosmic Unity', underlying the physical diversity that we experience in the world. The central quest of Indian spirituality is to achieve total experience of the One – the origin and end of all existence.

The One is made up of the primordial female energy of Shakti, whose essential nature is to be active and creative, embodying the energy and rhythm of life; and of Shiva, the male principle, identified with cosmic consciousness, the static pervasiveness of all phenomena. Creation is said to be the result of the creative play between the female and male energies of Shakti and Shiva. Although they seem to be polar opposites, they are essentially identical and inseparable. They are, together, the embodiment of unity and oneness. There can be no Shiva without Shakti, and no Shakti without Shiva, which strongly suggests that each of us carries an aspect of the opposite sex within us.

The yantra is a sacred Hindu mandala, a power diagram and meditative tool.

The yantra's geometric web

The 'yantra', a Hindu form of the mandala, is a potent sacred symbol, a power diagram and a meditative tool for attaining realization of the One. It is often compared to the spider in her web. Like the spider's web, the yantra is a geometric form, which takes the meditator toward its centre in stages, until his or her spiritual journey is complete. The concentric forms of the yantra function as bridges between different planes of existence, and contain the unfolding and gathering spiritual energies of the meditator. Each element of the yantra has many different levels of meaning and can be approached in different ways. All yantras encourage the meditator to achieve self-transcendence or enlightenment. However, you need a map to the layers of meaning in a yantra, otherwise its complexities will remain hidden from you. Without a map, the yantra remains a static, flat image rather than a dynamic process unfolding into layers of intricacy and beauty. This opening up or unfolding may happen by means of meditation on the yantra.

The Hindu Shri Yantra

The Shri Yantra is considered the most powerful and mystically beautiful. It represents the timeless creative principle of the universe, and the continuous unfolding of all realms of creation from the central source.

The central point of the Shri Yantra, called a *bindu*, represents the source of creation. The opposing sets of triangles represent the male and female principles that form creation out of the duality that is inherent in the creative force of the *bindu*. The upward-facing triangle symbolizes Shiva, the masculine force, and the downward-facing triangles symbolize Shakti, the feminine force. The surrounding forms of the yantra represent the realms of creation that are the result of their union. In Hindu thought, the universe would not exist without the omnipresence of the transcendental source represented by the *bindu*.

Lalita Tripurasundari

Every yantra is dedicated to a particular deity or archetype, and the Shri Yantra is presided over by Lalita Tripurasundari, also known as the 'Red Goddess'. *Lalita* means 'she who plays'. All creation, manifestation and dissolution are considered to be the play of the goddess. She symbolically occupies the centre of the Shri Yantra.

The yantra is arranged in concentric circles, called mandalas, which contain aspects of the goddess. The Shri Yantra has nine mandalas containing 111 aspects of Lalita Tripurasundari. The Shri Yantra is said to be a geometric representation of the human body, which implies that the goddess and human beings are one and that we embody her divinity within us. The nine mandalas of the Sri Yantra offer us the opportunity to experience Shakti-Shiva united as the One.

Lalita Tripurasundari has three aspects: the young one, the beautiful one and the terrible one. In her three forms she represents the three phases of the Hindu cosmic process: creation, preservation and dissolution.

According to Hindu philosophy, whatever is born will develop, age and dissolve again into the primordial reality that gave it life.

The Shri Yantra is the yantra of the Red Goddess Lalita Tripurasundari, also known as 'she who plays'.

The Earth square

The square, exterior limit of the Shri Yantra symbolizes the Earth. Every yantra emanates from the *bindu* at the centre and ends with the outer Earth square, which is represented as a city with four gateways. Outside

167

the gateways lie four very poetic oceans: the sugarcane ocean of duty, the salt ocean of wealth, the ghee ocean of bliss, and the milk or wine ocean of Liberation.

The Earth city, or Earth square, has three bands, showing that it is composed of three layers. At the outer layer the meditator visualizes meeting the eight gods who promote confidence through their protection. Next, at the middle layer of the Earth square, he or she finds *siddhis*. *Siddhis* are often described as 'superhero' attributes, such as flying through the air or becoming invisible. But you can think of them is as metaphors for strengths that you already have but don't recognize – your personal *siddhis* are discovered by going deep within yourself.

The *siddhis* of the middle layer of the Earth square are smallness, bigness, heaviness, lightness, quickness, wilfulness, creativity and subjugation. These powers do not have a fixed meaning – you decide what

The Indian goddess Lalita is said to be extremely merciful and to lead devotees to liberation.

they mean to you. For example, *smallness* may suggest allowing yourself to feel vulnerable and fearful, rather than suppressing those feelings. *Bigness* could be described as bigness of heart, allowing others to have their faults and insecurities without judging them. *Heaviness* could mean holding your ground when necessary without being defensive. *Lightness* suggests walking lightly on the Earth. *Quickness* could mean being fast and efficient in obtaining your objective. *Wilfulness* suggests a positive quality of being focused on what you want. *Creativity* is whatever that word means to you. And *subjugation* suggests the ability to suppress negative thinking or habits that get in the way of being your true self.

The inner layer of the Earth square represents desire, anger, greed, delusion, euphoria/smugness, jealousy, merit and demerit. (Merit and demerit refer to ordinary or confusing activities respectively.) The challenge here is to not be judgmental or demoralized about your negative emotions, or hard on yourself for any weakness. Emotions are manifestations of your humanity and have the potential to be transformed into aspects of wisdom.

The mandala of 16 petals

Meditatively you now enter the city by passing the guardians of the gateways and moving inward, where you encounter the first ring of lotus petals. This mandala of 16 petals is called the 'Fulfiller of Desire'. This mandala is associated with the attainment of desires by cultivating strength or power over the 16 aspects of your body and the world that keep you caught up in your ego, and that prevent you from furthering your spiritual knowledge.

The 16 petals represent the ways through which we experience and explore the world around us and express ourselves. Starting in the west and moving anti-clockwise they are: earth, air, fire, water, space, ear, skin, eye, tongue, nose, speaking, hands, feet, anus, sexual organs and wandering mind. The 16 petals represent the elements and aspects of our bodies through which we explore our surroundings and express ourselves. It is important here to recall that Lalita, the Red Goddess, represents a playful approach to life. If possible, refrain from judgmental or puritanical feelings when considering your 16 aspects. Simply acknowledge that loosening the grip that these aspects have over your body and mind could open you to new realizations and insights.

The eight petals

The next eight petals represent:
1 Speech and expression
2 Apprehension and receptivity
3 Locomotion
4 Bodily urges such as excretion
5 Pleasure
6 Rejection
7 Acceptance and detachment
8 Dispassion

They relate closely to the 16 petals. If the 16 petals are your vehicles for exploration, then the eight petals are those things that you explore and experience. Your experiences become alive through your senses, and through them you become awake and aware. You start to realize that everything around you is connected to you, through you and with you. The Shri

The Hindu deity Shiva, the transformer principle of the Hindu trinity, is seated here in meditation.

Yantra represents the totality of your experience and helps you achieve a state of energized, awake awareness; it changes your perception of the world.

The Shri Yantra is about being human, with all your faults and failings. It is not about achieving perfection, or becoming detached from the world as an idealized and remote spiritual being. Rather, it is meant to help you accept who you are, and work with what you have. It helps you see how your habits have limited you, and how your body may be armoured and cut off from feeling. It invites you to accept yourself with compassion, and alter those aspects of yourself that are holding you back, if you wish.

As you move into the various layers of the Shri Yantra, which are outlined in greater detail in the following exercise, they become more abstract – that is, until you reach the *bindu*, the centre of the yantra. At this point, you will begin to see the world differently, beyond ordinary perception.

The Hindu goddess Shakti, consort of Shiva, shown with many arms and hand implements, symbols of her vast powers.

Meditation on the Shri Yantra can help you awaken aspects of your emotional and physical self.

If you gaze at the Shri Yantra for a period of time, it may begin to vibrate or pulsate. You may feel this energy envelop your body, and begin to awaken aspects of your emotional or physical self that have felt numb or deadened. Meditation on the Shri Yantra is a highly beneficial method of becoming aware of these blocks, and it offers a gentle way to address them within the loving container the Shri Yantra provides. Over time you can release the armouring that prevents you from fully experiencing life.

173

Exercise The Shri Yantra as a meditation on cosmic consciousness

You will find an outline of the Shri Yantra to colour on page 321. It is recommended that you photocopy and enlarge it. Study the image of the Shri Yantra on page 167 before you begin this meditative exercise.

1 First, focus on the three aspects of the square periphery of the Shri Yantra. As you colour it at the first layer, contemplate asking for protection; at the second layer, meditate on the strengths you already have but do not recognize; and at the third layer, contemplate the obstacles to your spiritual development, such as worldly desire, anger, greed or jealousy.

2 Next, focus on the 16 petals that represent the 16 different aspects of your body and of the world that may keep you caught up in your own ego, and prevent you from furthering your spiritual knowledge. They are the five elements (earth, water, fire, air and space) and the ten sense organs (the ears, skin, eyes, tongue, nose, mouth, feet, hands, arms and genitals) plus the dualistic mind.

Meditation on the Shri Yantra provides a journey into the deepest aspects of yourself and the cosmos.

As you colour them, contemplate their meaning. But, most importantly, celebrate your sensual self and gently explore those areas of body or mind where you may be blocked. Stop colouring for a few minutes, close your eyes and breathe into every part of your body, starting with your toes and moving up to the top of your head. Notice any feelings that arise. When you are ready, open your eyes and continue colouring.

3 Now turn your attention inward to the ring of eight petals. These represent additional obstacles to your spiritual development, such as negative speech, the tendency to grasp after things, and

approaching everything in life with attachment, aversion or indifference. Meditate on how these limitations affect your spiritual growth. Meditate also on how they make you human. Fill your heart with love and compassion for yourself as you are.

4 Now, focus on the outer 14 triangles that represent aspects of your subtle body. According to the Hindu tradition, your body has energy channels through which your vital energy flows. If you cannot feel the channels, simply acknowledge that you have them.

5 Moving inward, focus on the next ten triangles. These represent various vital energies that flow through the channels of your body. Meditate on the fact that you are not just a physical being, but also an energetic being.

6 Moving inward yet again, you will find another ring of ten triangles. These represent the ten functions of prana, or vital energy. Visualize prana as it moves through your body, making it possible for you to live.

7 The next ring is made up of eight triangles. Three of them represent the three principles of nature according to Hindu tradition: Sattva, associated with purity, intelligence and calmness of mind; Rajas, the force behind creation, expressed as passion, egotism and restlessness; and Tamas, equated with inertia and expressed as resistance to change. Meditate on these aspects and how they manifest in your life.

8 You have now arrived at the innermost triangle. Meditate here on the fact that your normal understanding of the world is dualistic, in which you falsely perceive the separateness of subject and object, of yourself from others.

9 Finally, you have arrived at the small dot, the bindu, at the centre of the Shri Yantra, symbolizing your innermost self. Now meditate on your self as a whole, and as one with everything in the universe. Focus on the bindu and then expand to the entire mandala. Maintain this meditation for as long as you wish.

10 When you feel ready, end your meditation. Spend as long as you like writing about the Shri Yantra in your Mandala Journal, including the effect this meditation had on you and any other insights you may have gained.

A Hindu illustration of the subtle body, made up of chakras and energy channels through which vital energy flows.

Buddhist mandalas

Buddhists in China, Japan and Tibet create mandalas as tools for enlightenment. Of all the Eastern traditions, Tibetan Buddhism has made the most extensive use of the mandala.

Tibetan mandalas

The mandala in Vajrayana Buddhism depicts the sacred world and dwelling place of the Buddha or an enlightened being. At a minimum, Tibetan mandalas are made up of an outer ring, an inner circle or square and a mandala palace at the centre where the deity resides. When completed, the mandala becomes a sacred area that serves as an abode for a deity or deities, and as a collection point of universal forces. When the meditator visualizes entering the mandala and proceeding to its centre, he or she is guided symbolically through the cosmos to the essence of reality.

The outer circle of the Tibetan mandala represents separation and protection from the everyday or *samsaric* world – the world of suffering and eternal reincarnation. It often depicts a protective ring of fire, symbolizing the purifying fire

of wisdom. The inner circle or circles depict the stages of the spiritual path that a practitioner goes through on his or her journey to full realization. The centre represents the achievement of enlightenment, which is often depicted as a Buddha or enlightened being. Practitioners mentally visualize entering the mandala and becoming one with the Buddha residing in the centre. In this way they practise being enlightened.

In Tibetan Buddhism, contemplation of sacred images forms a focal part of religious ritual, and one of the most important sacred images is a mandala. A Tibetan mandala painted on cloth and surrounded with brocade is known as a *thangka*. Some mandalas are created on a flat surface with careful placement of coloured sands. In China, Japan and Tibet mandalas are sometimes made as three-dimensional figures.

Contemplation of sacred images, such as the mandala, is an integral part of Tibetan Buddhist practice.

The symbolism of Tibetan Buddhist mandalas

In Buddhism, mandalas are filled with symbols that represent aspects of the Buddha's teachings. When a monk creates a mandala, he does so while meditating on its meaning. Each mandala is different, depending on the deity or teachings represented, but certain aspects are repeated.

The outermost circle

All Tibetan mandalas begin with a dot in the centre, and the outer circle is made of stylized flames, which represents a ring of fire. This ring of fire reminds the meditator that spiritual transformation and purification are required before they are mentally able to enter the sacred space. The fire symbolically prevents the uninitiated from entering, and represents the burning away of ignorance.

The other circles

The next circle inward is a ring of *dorjes*, or small ritual sceptres made of diamonds, which signify the indestructible quality of enlightenment. Moving inward again, there is a circle of eight graveyards, which represent eight aspects of the mind that obstruct

the path to enlightenment. Finally, in many mandalas the innermost ring is made of lotus petals, representing spiritual awakening. The lotus grows in the dark mud, from which it emerges as a beautiful, luminous flower. It symbolizes the progress of the soul from the primeval mud of samsara, into the sunshine of enlightenment.

The square temple

In the centre of the mandala is a square temple where the deity resides. In the Tibetan tradition there are many male and female deities, but they are all manifestations or archetypes of the enlightened mind of Shakyamuni Buddha, the Buddha of our time. The temple's four gates symbolize the four immeasurables – love, compassion, joy and equanimity – and the four cardinal directions – south, north, east and west.

Within the square palace or temple, besides the main deity, are images of the Five Wisdom Buddhas. Each of these represents a direction (centre, south, north, east and west), a cosmic element (such as form or consciousness), an earthly element (space, air, water, earth and fire), and a particular type of wisdom that forms the antidote to a particular kind of delusion, such as ignorance, jealousy or hatred.

The image of the deity is placed over the centre dot, which is considered the centre of the universe.

Amitaba, the Buddha of Infinite Light, is one of five Wisdom Buddhas. He transmutes passion into spiritual energy.

The Buddhist Wheel of Life mandala

The Wheel of Life mandala is a little different from the Buddhist mandala already described, in that it is a teaching mandala. Its purpose is to illustrate the essence of all the Buddha's teachings, which is contained in his Four Noble Truths.

The Noble Truths the Buddha taught are:
• Life is suffering
• The cause of suffering is attachment and desire
• It is possible to end suffering
• There is a path that can lead to liberation.

The Four Noble Truths describe the causes of suffering as experienced by everyone from the cradle to the grave. They remind us that we are responsible for our own fate, because – according to the laws of karma – what we experience in life is the consequence of our actions, whether from this life or previous lives. The Wheel of Life mandala, which is based on the Four Noble Truths, is a teaching tool for those who have yet to experience the first step of spiritual liberation – the attainment of Nirvana. It depicts the Buddhist view that all living beings are caught in an endless cycle of death and rebirth.

Composition of the Wheel of Life

The Wheel of Life is best understood as five teaching narratives arranged in concentric circles. Starting in the centre, at the hub of the Wheel, three animal icons signify the basis of our human fallibility. The pig symbolizes ignorance, the snake represents anger and the cock stands for pride. They are biting each other's tails to demonstrate how these negative emotions are inseparably connected. The pig, snake and cock are drawn against a blue sky, signifying the spacious, pure nature of our human mind and our potential for enlightenment. The mandala reminds

The Wheel of Life mandala is held by Yama, the Lord of Death, teaches the Buddha's Four Noble Truths.

us that our real nature – our Buddha-nature – is obscured by our delusions.

Around the hub is a circle, which is half white and half black, showing human bodies descending and rising. This represents the results of our karma – in other words, the consequences of our good and bad actions. On the light side, our positive actions result in good karma and

The centre of the Wheel of life mandala shows three animals that symbolize the three major delusions.

rebirth in the higher realms; on the dark side, our negative actions result in rebirth in the lower realms. Moving outward from the black and white circle representing karma is a larger divided circle in six sections, which represent the six 'realms of existence' into which one can be reborn. These six realms also signify six habitual psychological attitudes that we embody in our daily lives.

The outer rim depicts 12 scenes of ordinary events in life, beginning not with our birth, but with our spiritual ignorance. Finally, Mara (or Death) embraces the Wheel from behind, to remind us that we will all have to face death sooner or later. The positive imagery of the symbols serves to encourage our positive actions, while the negative imagery aims to remind us that negative actions and behaviour are the root cause of our suffering.

The circular composition of the Buddhist Wheel of Life guides the viewer through the 12 interwoven causes and their consequences, to rebirth in one of the Six Realms of existence. But the meaning of this mandala is symbolized in traditional paintings by the figure beyond the mandala pointing to the moon, who shows us that there is a way out of all these worlds of suffering, by practising the path of the Buddha.

Next we will explore each of the Six Realms of rebirth and the 12 causes and their consequences in greater detail.

The Six Realms of Buddhist rebirth

According to Buddhists, when we are reborn, we are born into one of these Six Realms. The realm into which we are reborn is considered to be a result of our karma in our previous life. Rebirth as a human being – although filled with suffering – is considered the best rebirth because it is the only realm in which we can develop spiritually, escape from the wheel of endless rebirths and enter Nirvana.

1 If we are reborn into the *human* realm, our main problem is attachment and desire throughout our entire life.

2 If we are reborn as an *animal*, we are consumed by fear. If we are not hunting or being hunted by other animals, we may be used and abused by humans.

3 In the realm of karmic *hell* – the third place where we can be reborn – we face the consequences of the negative karma generated by the three poisons in our former life.

4 If we are reborn into the *hungry ghost* realm, our life will be nothing but greed and stinginess. In this realm

In the fifth realm, the realm of the demigod, we are ruled by jealousy and covet what others have.

A green jade statue of the Buddha appears in front of a Buddhist Wheel of Life mandala.

we feel we are never satisfied, and there is never enough.

5 The fifth realm is the realm of the *demigod*. This is the realm of jealousy. If we are reborn as a demigod, we will be consumed by coveting what others have and will be willing to go to war to get it. In the everyday world you might find demigods in cut-throat fields like high finance or banking, or among the upper echelons in the governments of aggressive countries.

6 In the sixth and final realm of Buddhist rebirth, the heavenly or *god* realm, we are completely blinded by pride. In this realm we think very highly of ourselves, as we reside in an exquisitely beautiful and comfortable place, surrounded by riches and living a life of ease. Yet, because of all this luxury, we have no motivation to work on our spiritual development. Eventually we will fall back into one of the lower realms.

Considering the Six Realms as psychological states

The most powerful way in which to contemplate the Six Realms is to consider them as psychological states. For example, it is possible to cycle through the Six Realms in one day, depending on the quality of your mind at any given moment.

As you arrive at work, your day feels like any other day. You feel like an ordinary *human* being. Then,

In the hungry ghost realm we feel a continual sense of loss, hunger and longing.

suddenly, you are seized with fear and become like an *animal* caught in the headlights. You learn from a co-worker that management has planned cutbacks and they are going to happen today. As the end of the day nears, your worst fear comes true. You are given notice that you are to clear your desk and leave. Then, as you walk dejectedly to the parking lot with your cardboard box of personal items, you discover that your car has been stolen. Your life is turned upside down and this makes you feel as if you have descended into the *hell* realms.

As you ride the subway home you begin to feel as if you are a failure, and that you will never get ahead. In your mind, you are a victim of your boss, and of the thief who is somewhere in the city driving your car. You have slipped into the realm of the hungry ghost. From this perspective you feel there is never really enough of anything in your life: not enough money, luck, love, sex, recognition, material possessions, respect or happiness. Your glass is always half empty.

The next morning you call your best friend to tell her the bad news and she

When we feel 'on top of the world', it is as if we are in the god realms.

tells you about her new promotion. You say that you are happy for her, but in reality, instead of rejoicing in her good fortune, you feel envious. Now you are in the realm of the *demigods*, also known as the 'jealous gods'. After you hang up, you begin to obsess about everything your friend has, including her beautiful apartment, prestigious job and handsome boyfriend. Unbelievably, you find yourself thinking about seducing her boyfriend at her party this weekend.

While lost in thoughts of jealousy and aggression, your ageing millionaire uncle rings you up with a spontaneous, last-minute invitation to go on a Mediterranean cruise that leaves tomorrow. Luckily you're free to go, because you no longer have a job. The next day you are catapulted from the demigod realm into the *god* realms, where you enjoy a first-class luxury cabin, gourmet food and a pampered existence. You are amazingly relaxed and happy for ten days. Your feelings of fear, neediness and jealousy fade as you look out

In each realm, a radiant buddha offers hope in the form of the Four Noble Truths.

contentedly over the vast blue sea. But of course the cruise comes to an end, and you fall from the god realms and return to your very human situation of having no job and no car.

It is easy to see how the Six Realms can be states of mind, and how we can inhabit all six in quick succession, even in the space of just one day. The Six Realms simply describe our human condition and the ways in which we suffer. Although it seems counter-intuitive, Buddhists consider the god realm a form of suffering because it is impermanent and does not provide the permanent happiness of enlightenment. According to the Buddha, nothing lasts – not even the joy of being on a luxury cruise. If you were on that cruise for years, day in and day out on the open seas, it could quickly transform into a prison, or a hell realm. And what appears to be a hell realm – having no job – could result in your finding the job of your dreams.

In each realm of existence in the Wheel of Life mandala you will find an image of a radiant Buddha offering hope. No matter what realm you find yourself in, or how difficult the

In the second panel, a potter creates pots symbolizing the results of our actions, or karma.

circumstances of your life at any given moment, or how much you are in the grip of negative emotions, the possibility of liberation is always present. Contemplating the Six Realms, and the ways in which you inhabit them, can help you to grow and mature in your personal and spiritual life and to understand the meaning of existence.

The 12 phases of human consciousness

The outer ring of the Wheel of Life mandala has 12 panels illustrating the 12 phases of human consciousness, also called the '12 links of inter-dependent origination'. They are to be read sequentially, clockwise, but each link connects to every other link. They are as follows:

1 In the first panel, at the top right, appears a spiritually blind man. In Buddhism, *ignorance* usually refers to ignorance of the Four Noble Truths.
2 Ignorance leads to *karma*. An image of a potter, whose pots represent

actions, symbolizes karma. We are responsible for the actions or 'pots' that we create in our life.
3 A monkey in a tree represents *consciousness*. The monkey symbolizes our 'monkey mind', or the constant chatter and continuously shifting thoughts of our untamed and untrained mind.
4 People travelling in a boat, rocking in the waves, symbolize *name and form*, the joining of body and mind into an individual existence, and our physical, intellectual or spiritual instability as we travel through life.
5 An empty house with six shuttered openings depicts the *six senses*: taste, touch, smell, sight, hearing and the conceptual mind. It also represents

In the fourth panel, people travel in a boat, rocking in the waves, symbolizing our instability as we travel through life.

the six corresponding *external objects*: visible form, sound, smell, taste, touch, and ideas and thoughts.

6 Two lovers embracing symbolize *contact* with the environment. Our senses give us the ability to feel and to experience the world.

7 A man with an arrow in his eye represents 'feeling', or the recognition and experience of *sensations*. Experience can be either pleasurable or painful, leading to attachment or aversion. The man also represents our tendency to categorize our feelings as pleasant, unpleasant or neutral.

8 A person drinking wine and dreaming of an object that he wants represents *craving* and the second Noble Truth: that desire or craving lies at the root of our suffering. The man's unrealized desires are stimulated by his emotions.

9 A monkey (or sometimes a person) picking fruit symbolizes *clinging or grasping*. We cling to sensual pleasures, mistaken ideas, external forms and appearances. Most of all we cling to ego and a sense of an individual self – a sense reinforced from moment to moment by our cravings and aversions.

10 An image of lovers (or a pregnant woman) symbolizes the pregnancy or new *becoming* that can result when we act on our cravings and desires.

11 A woman in childbirth symbolizes that the cycle of rebirth includes *birth*.

12 This frame depicts a corpse. Birth leads to *old age and death*, which are inevitable. Death does not end our suffering. We will begin a new cycle in the Wheel of Life. The karma of our life sets in motion our next life, which is also rooted in ignorance.

The Buddha's Four Noble Truths teach us that release from this cycle of ignorance, death and rebirth is possible. By working to transform our ignorance and craving into wisdom, our anger and hatred into love, and our pride and ego-grasping into compassion, we can achieve liberation from suffering and the peace of Nirvana.

Birth leads to old age and death, which are inevitable. Then we begin a new cycle in the Wheel of Life.

Exercise The Wheel of Life as a meditation on liberation from suffering

There is a simple *outline* of the Wheel of Life mandala on page 333. As you can see in the illustration on page 183, the actual Wheel of Life mandala is visually quite complex. For our purposes, the mandala is simplified to allow for ease of colouring and meditation; it can also be used as a template for painting your own Wheel of Life mandala.

1 Photocopy the Wheel of Life mandala on page 333 and enlarge it as much as possible onto the most substantial paper that the copier will accept (you may need to use a professional copy service). Alternatively, you can colour the mandala in this book.

2 Reread the explanation of the Wheel of Life mandala (see pages 182–195) and locate the various sections on the outline. Now begin colouring the mandala using paints or coloured pencils. As you colour each section, contemplate its meaning and apply that meaning to your own life. If you wish, you can add your own illustrations in the panels, or cut and paste modern images that represent the meaning of the various parts of the mandala for you.

3 Start colouring the centre of the mandala. As you do so, think of the root delusions of ignorance, anger and pride, and how they affect your life. Ask yourself if spiritual ignorance is present in your life. Does your current spiritual path serve you, or do you need to explore a different one? If at times you feel overcome by anger, think about ways in which to work with it and lessen its hold on you. Perhaps stop and concentrate on your breathing, if anger arises. If you are sometimes prideful and egotistical, think of how your pride harms you and of ways of focusing on caring for others.

A Chinese version of the Wheel of Life, called 'six ways of transmigration' or 'rebirth', Chongqing, China.

197

4 The next ring is divided into dark and light, representing positive and negative actions. As you colour it, meditate on both your positive actions and behaviours and your negative habitual patterns. Perhaps you are a good parent, but you overeat to the point of harming your health. Or you are kind to your co-workers, but sometimes take out your frustrations on your spouse. Think of ways in which to accentuate the positive and eliminate the negative in your life. Contemplate that all your thoughts and actions have consequences, and try to become more conscious of your behaviour. Try to do this with compassion and caring for yourself, and without feelings of shame or guilt.

5 Next, refresh your knowledge of the Six Realms (see pages 185–192). As you colour each realm, think of how you cycle through the Six Realms in your life. Feel free to draw images in the panels representing the realms that express their meaning for you. We often say 'I'm feeling human again' after a long illness, suggesting a sense of balance and well-being. How often do you feel balanced and that sense of well-being? When do you feel your animal fears arise? What triggers your fears? What are you afraid of? What feels like hell for you? When have you felt intense suffering? The 'hungry ghost' is a familiar mindset in modern life. Do you feel that you are never satisfied with the person you are, or what you have in life? If so, consider practising gratitude as an antidote. How often does jealousy strike? What triggers you to enter the demigod realms? What makes you feel as if you have entered the god realms? A holiday at a resort? A promotion? Romantic love? How do you feel when the inevitable fall to the lower realms occurs?

6 Finally, finish your mandala by reviewing, as you colour, the 12 phases of human consciousness (see pages 192–195) – the 12 panels that present a narrative of how we journey through life.

7 Hang up your completed mandala and think of three ways in which you can overcome your negative attitudes and emotions, and three ways in which you can bring more positive energy into your life.

Meditation on the Buddhist Wheel of Life mandala can provide you with spiritual guidance and inspiration.

EXERCISE THE WHEEL OF LIFE AS A MEDITATION ON LIBERATION FROM SUFFERING

Christian mandalas

In the 6th century CE Pope Gregory the Great asked that Catholic dogma be represented in symbol and image on the walls of churches for the benefit of the uneducated faithful. And a papal Synod in 1025 reiterated that illiterate members of congregations must be given a way to learn the teachings of the Church.

The first Christian mandalas were round frescos and wall paintings. These powerful images were the precursors to the giant rose windows that appeared in France following the Crusades. The first rose windows appeared around the year 1200.

Western stained-glass rose windows in churches and cathedrals have been a source of great beauty and inspiration throughout the centuries. Like Buddhist and Hindu mandalas, the Christian rose window represents an aspiration to wholeness and transformation. It functions on various levels: spiritual, meditative and emotional. Upon entering a dark Gothic cathedral with its soaring interior, the viewer is struck – and often deeply moved – by the beauty of the light streaming through the jewel-like glass. Looking at the rose window can evoke an emotional experience, transporting the viewer from ordinary consciousness to spiritual realization. Simply following the tracery with the eye and taking in the patterns found

Like Eastern mandalas, the Christian rose window represents an aspiration to wholeness and transformation.

The north rose window at Chartres Cathedral, France, 'Glorification of the Virgin'.

in a rose window can induce a calm or meditative mood.

Like Eastern mandalas, the rose window functions as a spiritual map or blueprint. Contained within it are teachings on how to bring one's ordinary life closer to God. The instructional aspect of rose windows is plainly visible in the symbols and images in each part of it. Themes included the story of creation, astrological signs and symbols, and symbols of the Catholic Church, such as the Agnus Dei or Lamb of God, and the orb surmounted by a cross.

201

The west rose window of Notre-Dame Cathedral, Paris

The west rose window is the oldest of the three rose windows of Paris's Notre-Dame Cathedral. Constructed around 1220 CE, it is an impressive 10 m (33 ft) in diameter.

The upper half of the circle depicts the virtues and vices, and the lower half, the Labours of the Months and the signs of the Zodiac. The innermost ring of the window contains the 12 prophets, and at the centre is the Virgin Mary.

To those living in the medieval era, God created the universe and animated everything in it. Reality was ordered and hierarchical, with God at the pinnacle of existence. Daily life was deeply rooted in the cycles of nature. Ordinary people used the 12 signs of the Zodiac, combined with the Labours of the Months, to keep track of time; both were used to decorate churches and public buildings. The charming scenes of the Labours of the Months depict seasonal agricultural tasks that were instantly recognizable to medieval congregations.

The Zodiac

Despite its pagan origins, the Zodiac was in widespread use in Christian medieval life. Ordinary people looked to the night sky to understand the present, predict the future and mark the passage of time. Because most were engaged in agriculture, the movements of planets and constellations helped forecast the weather and decide the times for planting and other activities. Astrological divination was a common part of everyday life. The 12 constellations that form the Zodiac are: Aries (the Ram), Taurus (the Bull), Gemini (the Twins), Cancer (the Crab), Leo (the Lion), Virgo (the Virgin), Libra

The West rose window of Notre-Dame Cathedral, Paris, is dedicated to the Virgin Mary.

(the Scales), Scorpio (the Scorpion), Sagittarius (the Archer), Capricorn (the Goat), Aquarius (the Water Bearer) and Pisces (the Fish).

In the medieval mind, the 12 signs of the Zodiac influenced everything in life. For example, the signs were thought to rule various parts of the human body: the Ram ruled the head; the Bull, the throat and neck; the Twins embraced the shoulders; the Crab ruled the breasts and stomach; the Lion, the heart and back; the Virgin, the nervous system and the bowels; the Scales, the lower back; the Scorpion, the sexual organs; the Archer, the thighs; the Goat, the knees; the Water Bearer, the shins and ankles; and the Fish, the area under the feet. In other words, the Zodiac played a role in the practice of medicine.

The Signs of the Zodiac also extended into the rest of physical reality: the seasons, the ages of life, the elements, winds, qualities, conditions, humours, temperament and colours. To the medieval person,

In the medieval mind, each Zodiac sign was thought to rule part of the body. Sagittarius, the archer, ruled the thighs.

all existence was alive and animated. This merging of pagan beliefs and Catholic dogma is recorded in the stained glass of Notre-Dame's west rose window.

The Labours of the Months

In a Gothic cathedral, the Labours of the Months show the ordinary world of work – the world that medieval persons inhabited on a daily basis, which was set aside when they entered the cathedral for worship. Because the Labours were most often depicted on the west facade of the church, they appear in the west rose window at Notre-Dame. According to Christian theology, manual labour began when Adam and Eve were ejected from the Garden of Paradise. So the Labours not only show people in their ordinary lives at work, but also remind the faithful of the consequences of Original Sin. When crossing the threshold of the church, people are encouraged to leave the everyday world of sin behind and to embrace the blessings and divine grace to be found within.

Gothic style is based on logical thought. The medieval person believed that God created each thing separately in its place, so Gothic art and architecture reflect this way of thinking. By showing the 12 months and their respective Labours, along with the Zodiac, the stained-glass artist created a rational and orderly design. The west window would have been very accessible to the faithful as it shows a set of familiar events, labours, virtues and vices, which are all depicted in an understandable and memorable sequence.

The Labours of the Months demonstrate the medieval peasant at work, but even for the wealthy and for merchants, the calendar was still determined by the cycles of the Zodiac and the agricultural seasons. But unlike solar and astrological time, the message of Christ is linear: it has a beginning and an end, including His sacrifice on the cross and Resurrection.

The illustrations of the Labours of the Months are as follows:

January A man is shown with two drinking horns, which depict the Roman god Janus with two heads, looking in opposite directions. Janus symbolizes the ending of one year and the beginning of another.

February In northern climates during the winter months, agricultural work comes to a standstill, so a man is seen sitting in front of the fire.

March This is the time to trim vines in France, so a peasant is shown either trimming or digging.

April The return of spring and new crops is a cause for dancing and rejoicing. A youth celebrates and wears a crown of flowers.

May The traditional month of courtly love shows a knight on horseback or a peasant resting in the shade.

June This is the month for working in the fields, mowing the meadows, hay-making and sheep-shearing.

July At the beginning of the harvest a peasant cuts the crop with a sickle.

August The harvest continues in late summer, and the peasant strips down to work in the heat.

September This is the time to pick grapes, make wine and gather fruit.

October The wine is poured into casks, and the peasants prepare the fields for next year.

The Labours of the Months showed that the medieval calendar was determined by agricultural seasons.

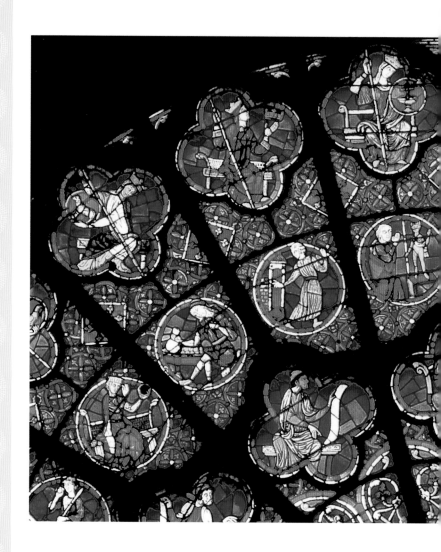

November A peasant is shown fattening his pigs on acorns.
December The pigs are killed and cakes are baked for the Christmas celebration.

Virtues and vices

Every spiritual tradition provides guidance on how to live a moral and virtuous life, and the Catholic faith is no exception. The medieval Catholic Church provided moral guidance to its members to help ensure a stable society, and to provide a path to God for the true spiritual seeker.

The upper half of Notre-Dame's west rose window depicts 12 virtues and their corresponding vices for the viewer to contemplate. The lower half of the window roots the Church's teachings in the everyday, while the upper half invites the viewer to monitor his or her thoughts and behaviour, so as to bring one's ordinary life closer to God.

The vices and antidote virtues paired in the west rose window are: Pride and Humility, Folly and

The west rose window guides the faithful on how to live a virtuous life.

Prudence, Lust and Chastity, Avarice and Charity, Inconstancy and Perseverance, Idolatry and Faith, Anger and Patience, Despair and Hope, Ingratitude and Gentleness, Discord and Peace, Rebellion and Obedience, Cowardice and Strength.

The 12 Minor Prophets

The inner ring of the west rose window, the one that is closest to the centre, depicts the 12 Minor Prophets. They are considered 'minor' because their writings are shorter that those of Isaiah, Jeremiah, Ezekiel and Daniel. Yet the contents of their prophecies were as powerful and moving as those of the four Major Prophets. Prophets were thought to be channels of the Holy Spirit, which enabled the word of God to flow through them.

The Minor Prophets are the authors of the 12 short prophetic texts that are included within the Hebrew Bible as well as the Christian Old Testament. Their writings span Israelite/Jewish history over hundreds of years, from the Assyrian period to the Persian. Because their prophecies spread out over many centuries, they addressed the Jews in different circumstances – from those suffering and wandering in exile, to the enthusiastic builders of a permanent Temple. The Minor Prophets stressed that, no matter what they were going through, the Israelites were God's chosen people and should behave as if they were. In this way the Prophets connect with the teachings on the virtues and vices in the upper half of the window. The Prophets emphasize devotion to God and remind that God will act in the future to reward the faithful and punish the wicked.

The 12 Minor Prophets are:

Hosea, using the sexist metaphor of his day, described God as the suffering husband of Israel, whose citizens were collectively portrayed as His dallying wife.

Joel delivered the message that transgressions against God have consequences at the end of life.

Amos, the first of the biblical prophets, denounced the immorality of both Israel and its contemporaries.

Obadiah warned the Edomites that they would face God's wrath for destroying the Temple and mistreating the Judeans.

Jonah warned the sinful people of Nineveh that they would face judgment, and caused them to repent.

Micah shamed the economic elites in Judean society for their religious hypocrisy.

Nahum celebrated the collapse of the Assyrian empire, which persecuted the Jews.

Habakkuk warned that the Kingdom of Judah would fall if its residents did not return to the law of Moses.

Zephaniah predicted divine judgment against Jerusalem and Judah, as well as divine protection.

Haggai prophesied that continued existence of the Jewish people (and the Jewish faith) depended upon the reconstruction of the Temple.

Zechariah underscored the necessity for a homeland and a Temple for Jewish nationhood, and devotion to Yahweh in order for the nation to remain in existence.

Malachi criticized the temple priests for being lax, and the laity for not paying tithes.

Adorning the exterior of the west rose window is a statue of the Virgin with Child standing between two angels.

Mary as compassionate protector

In the centre of this decidedly masculine mandala, which teaches morality through fear of judgment, resides the compassionate and accepting Mother Mary with Christ Child. She humanizes both the Church's teachings on morality and the harsh warnings of the Old Testament prophets, and gives hope to those who struggle to live up to the path that is laid out for them. She offers to intercede for the faithful in their desire to approach God, and offers compassionate protection as they strive to live a moral life. When the father is harsh, it is natural to turn to the more accepting and forgiving mother.

The earliest known prayer to Mary, composed in the 4th century CE, is the *Sub tuum praesidium*, which is Latin for 'under your protection'. It begins with the words 'Beneath your compassion, we take refuge.' Artistic depictions of the Virgin Mary often portray her in the role of the protector

Mary as compassionate protector resides in the centre of the west rose window of Notre-Dame Cathedral.

of Christians, as she shelters them under her mantle, sometimes from a rain of arrows from above. From ancient times the Blessed Virgin has been honoured with the title of 'Mother of God', to whose protection the faithful turn amid all their problems and needs. Other titles are 'Mother of Sorrows' or 'one who understands and shows compassion'. Mary's popularity expanded dramatically in the Middle Ages, and Catholics have continued to this day to seek the protection of Mary and have relied on her intercession as 'Queen of Heaven'.

The Catholic prayer known as the *Memorare* combines the protection of the Virgin Mary with her role of interceding with God on behalf of the faithful: 'Never was it known that anyone who fled to Thy protection, implored Thy help or sought Thy intercession was left unaided.'

During the 15th century St Louis de Montfort further elevated the stature of Mary by teaching that God appointed her to dispense Grace to the faithful. He introduced the idea that Grace from God can come through the Blessed Virgin.

Exercise A rose window for Mary, Queen of Heaven

There is a simplified outline of the west rose window of Notre-Dame Cathedral on page 345 (and a key to its various elements is given below), although the actual west rose window is visually complicated.

Below is a key to the stained-glass elements of the window for you to use as you colour – it indicates where to find the signs of the Zodiac and their corresponding Labours and the virtues and vices. The Prophets are located in the keyed drawing, but the exact location of each Prophet is not known. When colouring this section, simply choose where you wish to locate each Prophet in the areas designated for Prophets in the rose window.

KEY TO THE ROSE WINDOW'S ELEMENTS

1 Prophet	16 Discord	31 Pride	46 September
2 Prophet	17 Rebellion	32 Folly	47 August
3 Prophet	18 Cowardice	33 Lust	48 July
4 Prophet	19 Capricorn	34 Avarice	49 June
5 Prophet	20 Sagittarius	35 Inconstancy	50 May
6 Prophet	21 Scorpio	36 Idolatry	51 April
7 Prophet	22 Libra	37 Patience	52 March
8 Prophet	23 Virgo	38 Hope	53 February
9 Prophet	24 Leo	39 Gentleness	54 January
10 Prophet	25 Cancer	40 Peace	55 Humility
11 Prophet	26 Gemini	41 Obedience	56 Prudence
12 Prophet	27 Taurus	42 Strength	57 Chastity
13 Anger	28 Aries	43 December	58 Charity
14 Despair	29 Pisces	44 November	59 Perseverance
15 Ingratitude	30 Aquarius	45 October	60 Faith

Mary was thought of as protecting and defending the faithful, and interceding for them with God.

215

1 Before you begin, photocopy the mandala on page 345 and enlarge it as much as possible onto the most substantial paper that the copier can accept. Or you can colour the mandala in the book using coloured pencils. Alternatively, copy the mandala onto clear film, then use markers to colour it. When completed, hang your mandala in a window, where it will be illuminated like the original rose-window mandala.

2 Reread the explanation of the rose-window mandala (see pages 202–213) and locate the various sections on the outline. As you colour each section, contemplate its meaning and then apply that meaning to your own life.

3 Begin by colouring the outermost two rings of the lower half of the rose window. The outermost ring of closed forms represents the months, or signs of the Zodiac. As you colour, consider how you experience the passing of time and the seasons in your own life. Consider the power of the Zodiac and the ancient

The Zodiac had a powerful influence in medieval times. This image depicts the movement of the planets.

meanings of the signs. Spend extra time at your birth month and the current month. Are you aware of the cyclical changes in nature and in the constellations in the sky above?

4 Moving inward, the next ring of circles contains the 12 corresponding Labours of the Months. These may seem quaint and outdated, but on further reflection you may realize that you have your own modern-day

division of your labours. What activities occupy you in December, or in January, or in July? How are they different? Are you aware of the passing of the seasons, and do you plan any activities to honour and celebrate them?

5 Now move to the upper half of the rose-window mandala. The outer ring represents the 12 virtues, and the next, inner ring, their corresponding vices. As you colour these,

consider how they affect your life. Are some pairs of virtues and vices more interesting to you than others? For example, as a modern emancipated person you may have resistance to the notion of Obedience and Rebellion. On the other hand, Patience and Anger or Inconstancy and Perseverance may be issues that you want to contemplate. Procrastination is a more modern word for inconstancy, but it seems that the issue is universal and timeless for humankind.

Meditation on the west rose window will help you contemplate the passage of time, the passage of the seasons, and the cyclical changes in nature.

6 When you have completed both outer halves of the west rose window, move to the Prophets. Reread the information on the Prophets (see page 210) and, as you colour, consider their messages. How do you react to the challenges they present?

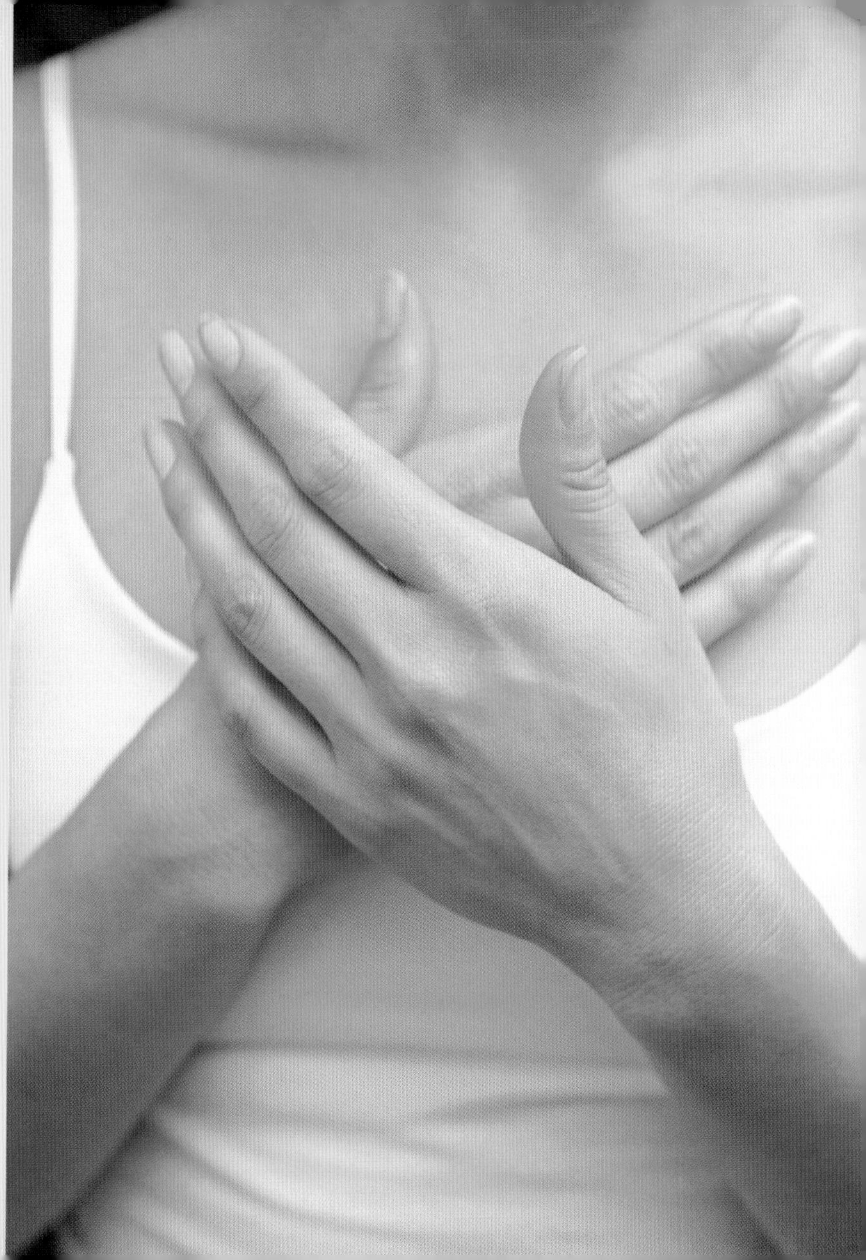

Do you feel galvanized by some of their messages and repelled by others? The authoritarian, harsh style of the Old Testament does not mesh well with modern life, but if you move beyond its style, there may be some things that it is useful to contemplate. For example, if you can get beyond Hosea's sexist metaphor, you may agree that our material culture in the West has rejected the true message of the major religions. Or if you believe in the power of karma, Joel's message is that there are consequences for our actions. Micah criticized religious hypocrisy, and it is easy to find modern examples in every culture. When considering the Prophets' messages as a whole, look at the priorities in your own life. What is truly important to you?

7 Finally you arrive at the centre of the rose mandala, where the Virgin Mary is enthroned. She embodies the central message of the west rose window, which is love and compassion. As you colour the centre of the rose, consider whether you are hard on yourself for not living up to the standards set for you by others – including the Church, your family, your teachers or peers. Determine whether you are critical of yourself for not meeting your own high standards. Then meditate on Mary as an all-loving mother figure, who accepts you completely as you are. Feel her unconditional love and forgiveness for any failures in your life, either real or imagined. If you struggle in your ordinary life (the lower half of the window) or fail to meet your spiritual aspirations (the upper half of the window), or are afraid of judgment or punishment for your transgressions (the Prophets), contemplate Mary as your protector and defender. She believes in you and will intercede for you in your relationship with God. She is a source of grace.

8 When you have completed your rose-window mandala, either hang it up on a wall or, if you coloured it on film, hang it in a window. Use your own personal rose window to meditate on the feminine, and on the power of love and compassion.

Mary embodies the central message of the west rose window, which is compassion for yourself and others.

Celtic mandalas

The Celtic mandala is a modern-day creation that incorporates the Earth-centred mysteries and mythology of the Celtic peoples. The Celts, an Indo-European people, inhabited large parts of Central Europe, Spain, Ireland and Britain between the 5th and 1st centuries BCE.

Queen Maeve seeking advice from a Druid, illustration from 'Cuchulain, The Hound of Ulster', by Eleanor Hull (1860–1935).

Reproduction of manuscript illuminations from the Book of Durrow, a 7th century gospel book.

Unlike Greek and Roman culture, Celtic society was predominantly rural and tribal. The Celts were animists and believed that everything in the natural world contained spirits, or divine entities, with which humans could establish a relationship. Power in life came from the 'Otherworld' – the realm of ancestors and the dead, and the dwelling place of the gods and other spirits. Many animals were considered sacred, and trees were believed to have special powers. Celtic symbols reflect a deep connection to the patterns and energies of the natural world.

Archeological evidence suggests that the Celts made offerings to their gods throughout the landscape, often in groves of trees or springs that were held to be sacred. Votive offerings were buried in the earth or thrown into springs, rivers or bogs. At times the Celts worshipped in temples and shrines, which throughout Celtic Europe were square structures made of wood, and in the British Isles were circular in design. Irish structures were larger than those at other Celtic sites, the most notable being the Hill of Tara in County Meath, the seat of Irish kings until the 6th century.

This Celtic illustration of a bird-and-knot pattern invites contemplation on our interdependence with nature.

Celtic design

The Celtic design motifs used in modern-day Celtic mandalas include lozenges, spirals, key patterns, animals and knots, all of which are found in traditional Celtic art. These mystical patterns and symbols, incorporated into contemporary mandala forms, invite meditation on the interconnectedness of everything in the universe.

On the feast of St Brigid, women in parts of Ireland today still make amulets called St Brigid's crosses. These consist of a diamond-shaped lozenge of straw woven around a little wooden cross. Every year the crosses are blessed by the priest and hung in houses for protection against fire and lightning, and in stables for the protection of the animals. The lozenge is an ancient Celtic female symbol

This zoomorphic Celtic design creates complex patterns from animal, bird and reptile forms.

representing the vulva or womb of the Great Mother, and St Brigid is a direct descendant of the pre-Christian goddess Brigid.

The Celtic people and their ancestors used the spiral symbol (see pages 44–45) to represent both the natural world and the spiritual mysteries of life. Some of the best examples of Neolithic Celtic spirals are found on the entrance to the

megalithic passage tomb at Newgrange in eastern Ireland. The three-pronged 'Spiral of Life' at the entrance symbolized the sacred cycle of birth, death and rebirth. The spiritual initiate would walk around the spiral-marked barrier into the labyrinth sanctuary, where he or she would then follow the interior path to its centre. There, Heaven and Earth were joined. The Celtic triskelion – a three-pronged spiral within a circle – is also said to represent the Triple Goddess (see pages 30–31) of the three ages of womanhood: virgin, mother and crone. It can also be seen to symbolize the three experiences of existence: our relationship with the Earth, with ourselves and with the divine.

Celtic key patterns are angular, interlocking key shapes that are, in effect, straightened spirals. The paths formed by the pattern are constructed on a diagonal grid and turn back on themselves at various angles, symbolizing the winding path of the labyrinth. The key pattern suggests a spiritual journey, whereby a seeker simultaneously moves toward his or her spiritual centre and toward that of the universe. At the centre of the labyrinth, called 'the navel' or *omphalos*, Heaven, Earth and self are experienced as one.

Celtic knot patterns form complete loops, with no beginning and no end. They vary from relatively simple to highly complex and are found on crosses, structures, manuscripts and other artefacts throughout the Celtic world. Celtic zoomorphic (or animal)

The Celtic cross – a cross, superimposed with circular mandala – has its roots in the pre-Christian era.

designs are similar in construction, but the patterns terminate in feet, heads or tails. The intricate looping of knot patterns suggests the inter-connectedness of all life, eternity and the mysteries of birth, death and reincarnation. The interwoven figures of people and animals symbolize the intimate connection that the Celts had with the natural world. Some knots were used as magical talismans for protection from earthly threats and evil spirits.

The Celtic cross

The Celtic cross – a cross super-imposed with a circular mandala form – has its roots in the pre-Christian, Celtic pagan era dating back to 5,000 BCE. Although its exact origins are unknown, it may be an early symbol of the Celtic god Taranis. In the earliest periods the cross was drawn entirely within the circle and was without decoration. Later, the cross became much larger, the arms were extended, and both circle and cross were

covered with elaborate decorative elements drawn from pre-Christian Celtic iconography, including knots, spirals and key patterns.

As a pagan symbol, the Celtic cross combines the female circle and the male cross, to form an image of fertility and sexual union. The cross was associated with the four cardinal points (north, south, east and west) and with the flow of time; the circle with the cycles of death and rebirth and, at the centre – where time stands still – with the point of entry into the Underworld.

The Celtic cross became an emblem of the Church when the Celts converted to Christianity. The cross then symbolized Christ's crucifixion, and the circle His resurrection and eternal life.

Contemporary Celtic spirituality

The moral/ethical code of modern Celtic pagans is based both on modern society and on ancient legal texts and other writings, including:

Summer solstice ritual based on traditional pagan practice and western mysticism, Brighton, UK.

- Respect for nature and Earth's creatures
- Honour
- Truthfulness
- Service to one's community
- Loyalty to one's friends, family and local community
- Hospitality
- Justice
- Courage

Celtic pagans divide the world into three realms, Land, Sky and Sea, and into three planes of existence, the

Ordinary World, the Otherworld and the Underworld. All realms and planes are understood to be interconnected and sacred. There are also three divisions in the Celtic pantheon: the Gods of the Upper Realm (sky), the Gods of the Middle Realm (land) and the Gods of the Lower Realm or Underworld (related to the sea). Most Celtic pagans worship three types of deities: personal deities for inspiration and guidance, tribal deities for group practice, and the deities and spirits of the land where they live. Ancestors and land spirits also play a vital role in Celtic paganism.

Most Celtic pagan rituals are held in a natural setting. The ritual site is carefully selected, and the spirits that inhabit the surroundings are invoked. Celtic pagan ritual involves meditation, visualization, singing and dancing, which help practitioners attune to the Earth and to one another. The focus of the ritual is not on enhancing wealth or worldly success, but on reconnecting the individual, and the community, with Spirit and Nature, so that they can live their lives in harmony with each other and the universe.

The foundation stones of Celtic culture – home and family – also formed the basis of their spirituality. For the ancient Celts the sanctity of the home, and strength of the family, provided the grounding for their religious life. Because they lived in a tribal culture, family and community were extremely important. For contemporary Celtic pagans, family includes both their immediate families and the extended family of their spiritual community.

Exercise Meditation on a Celtic knotwork mandala

Many contemporary Celtic mandalas include traditional knotwork designs, which encourage meditation on the mysteries of the universe. Celtic knotwork is a distinctively Irish form of art, first created by Irish Christian monks who came to Ireland around the 7th century CE to convert the pagan Celts to Christianity.

Their illuminated manuscripts of the Gospels, filled with intricate interlaced designs and knotwork, were based on illuminations from Eastern Christendom, notably the Byzantine and Coptic Churches. Their designs also reveal traces of many other influences from countries outside the Christian world, including Egypt, ancient Greece, Syria, ancient Persia and Armenia. Thus Irish knotwork was first conceived as spiritual practice.

Some of the best examples of Irish knotwork are found in illuminated manuscripts, such as the Book of Armagh, the Book of Durrow and the Book of Kells. These manuscripts are spectacular in their rich and amazingly complex ornamentation. Initial letters are filled with interlaced designs, which signify the inter-connection of everything. Rich swirls and complicated knotwork fill the empty areas of the letters, and the serifs are decorated with animal motifs, braids, chevrons, diamond spirals and birds.

The knotwork designs used in Celtic mandalas are constructed from one or many individual lines that form loops. As each generation of lines passes, the weave grows larger and more complex and curves back on itself, so that the next set of lines brings forth another loop. Celtic knots symbolize the ineffable, and express a sense of

A carpet page from the Book of Durrow, *ca. 660–80, which is held at Celtic Art Trinity College Library, Dublin, Ireland.*

oneness with the divine. They simultaneously portray the reality of an interconnected, never-ending cycle of life on Earth, in which everything is related in the fabric of time and space. As the lines of Celtic knots are interwoven, so we are interwoven with everything in the universe.

Celtic knotwork design suggests the interconnected, never-ending cycle of life on Earth.

This interlacing may also have functioned as protection against evil – and the more complex the interlacing, the more powerful that protection.

A Celtic mandala can be used as a powerful talisman to protect against negative energies.

1 Begin by photocopying and enlarging the Celtic mandala on page 359 so that it is at least 15 cm (6 in) across. Then choose your colouring materials. If possible, include metallic markers or pens to replicate the look of an illuminated manuscript. When you have prepared your mandala, find a place where you will not be disturbed for about an hour, then take a moment to meditate on your breath. With each out-breath you will reach a deeper sense of relaxation.

2 When you are ready to start working on your mandala, consider playing instrumental Celtic themed music in the background. This should feel soothing and help you set the correct ambience for this exercise; in no way should it be distracting.

3 Begin colouring the outside rim of the mandala, then colour the background behind the interlaced knotwork. As you colour the background, imagine a ground of existence that is vast and limitless, as a kind of stage upon which your life takes place. Imagine a clear blue luminous space

that goes on forever – that is so vast it is beyond imagination.

4 Next, move to one of the knotwork halves that make up the mandala and begin colouring it in a contrasting shade to the background. Follow it along, until it ultimately curves back onto itself to where you began. As you colour, visualize being one with the divine, in whatever way you define that word. Now imagine everything and everyone as a magnificent display of that divinity.

5 When you are ready, move on to the second half of the mandala. Meditate on how you are interconnected with everything and everyone else in the universe. Take a moment to look around you, where you are sitting, and feel yourself connected to everything in the space around you – the furniture, the plants, your clothes, your treasured possessions, your cat or dog or bird, if you have one.

6 After you have finished colouring your mandala, go over the lines with gold or silver metallic ink, so that it resembles a page from an illuminated manuscript. Take a moment to write in your Mandala Journal about your experience.

Native American mandalas

Native American mandalas appear in at least three different forms:
the medicine wheel, the dream catcher and the sand mandala.

The medicine wheel

Around 100 Native American medicine wheels have been identified throughout North America, including examples in South Dakota, Wyoming, Montana, Alberta and Saskatchewan. The phrase 'medicine wheel' was first applied to the Bighorn Medicine Wheel in Wyoming in the western United States, and the term 'medicine' refers to its religious or spiritual significance to Native American peoples.

The Bighorn Medicine Wheel was constructed around 700 years ago and continues to be an important sacred site for Native Americans. It is made simply of locally gathered rocks. A cairn, or pile of stones, forms the centre, which is about 3 m (10 ft) across and 0.6 m (2 ft) high. From there, 28 spokes radiate out to the rim of the wheel, which is approximately 24 m (80 ft) in diameter and 75 m (245 ft) in circumference. There are six smaller cairns along the rim.

The Bighorn Medicine Wheel aligns with the rising and setting sun of the summer solstice, and three stars: Aldebaran, Rigel and Sirius. The 28 spokes probably correspond with the days of the lunar month.

For centuries the Bighorn Medicine Wheel has been used by Crow youth for fasting and vision quests. Other Native Americans also go to Bighorn to make prayer offerings. Prayers are offered for healing, and for atonement for harm done to others and to Mother Earth. A number of great chiefs, including Chief Joseph of the Nez Perce, have prayed at the Bighorn Medicine Wheel.

The dream catcher

Dream catchers originated with the Ojibwe tribe of the Great Lakes region

A Navajo medicine man creates a sacred sand mandala using fine grains of coloured sand.

of the United States. While researching the Ojibwe in the year 1900 the anthropologist Frances Densmore (1867–1957) noticed something that looked like a spider's web hanging from the hoop of a child's cradleboard. She was told that it caught and held everything evil, just as a spider's web catches and holds everything that comes into contact with it. These 'dream catchers' were mandala-like wooden hoops with a 9 cm (3½ in) diameter, filled with a web made of nettle-stalk cord, which was dyed red with bloodroot and the inner bark of wild plum. A feather was traditionally placed in the centre of the dream catcher to symbolize breath, or air. The feather of the owl was used for wisdom (a woman's feather) and the feather of an eagle for courage (a man's feather).

A dream catcher can be hung above an adult's sleeping area, in a place where it will be bathed in morning light. It will attract dreams to its web: bad dreams will get caught in the web and the first light of day

Dream catchers for sale, Monument Valley Tribal Park, Utah, USA.

will cause them to melt away; good dreams, knowing the way through to the centre of the web, will slide down the feather to the sleeper below. The dream catcher will not get rid of bad dreams if they are important for the dreamer.

The hoop of the dream catcher is generally made of willow. And the web has at least seven points for the seven grandfathers (spirits provided by the Creator, who teach seven virtues), and sometimes 13 for the 13 moons, or 28 for the lunar month.

The sand mandala

The Navajo sand mandala, which is similar to the Tibetan mandala, depicts an ideal place or abode where deities or ideal beings dwell. Through ritual and imagination, the sand mandala becomes a sacred reality.

This Native American sand painting depicts Holy People interacting in a sacred world.

Hozho is a Navajo word that means 'harmony' – both gaining harmony and maintaining it. It means to 'walk in beauty' with a sense of rightness with the world. To be in true *hozho*, one must embrace the world and the environment, while maintaining a clear sense of one's authentic self. Sometimes, to restore a person's *hozho*, a *hataalii* – a Navajo healer, also known as a Singer or a Medicine Man – performs a sand-mandala ceremony. The *hataalii* incorporates the appropriate *yei* figure into the sand painting in or near the person's home (the *yei* is a Holy Person who allows communication between the Navajo and the gods).

In the Navajo tradition, the sand mandala depicts Holy People acting in the sacred world. Not shown in the painting (but understood to be present during the sand-painting ceremony) are certain Holy Persons in training – spiritual heroes or heroines for the Navajo to emulate. By identifying with the Holy People and the spiritual heroes or heroines, the person for whom the sand-mandala ritual is being held begins to take on the ideal thoughts and energies of the cosmos.

Navajos create their mandalas by sprinkling fine grains of coloured sand on top of a bed of sand in thin streams, from between thumb and index finger. Four or more sand painters are directed by the chanter. Sometimes the mandala is enhanced with flower petals, corn pollen or powdered semi-precious jewels. It can be rectangular or round. If it is round, the painters sit on the periphery and work from the centre outward to the four directions. The mandala transforms itself into the sacred space where the Holy People interact with the ritual's participants.

After the Holy People have been invoked, the subject is psychologically and physically brought into the centre of the mandala. Any illness is drawn out of that person into the sand. Through imagination, the one being sung over begins to transform his or her troubled body-mind. He or she begins to find balance within the ideal reality of the Holy People. The mandala is the symbolic vehicle for restoring the patient to the state of 'beauty'.

Once the ceremony is over, the sand mandala is ritually destroyed so that its power cannot be misused.

Exercise Ojibwe dream-catcher mandala

The Ojibwe dream catcher is related to the myth of Spider Woman and how she helped bring sun back to the tribe. It is told that Spider Woman builds her special lodge before dawn. At dawn, you will see how she captured the sunrise as the light sparkles on the dew of her web.

One of Spider Woman's roles is to take care of children. When the Ojibwe nation dispersed to the four corners of North America, she had a difficult time making her way to all those children. To help her, mothers, sisters and grandmothers began weaving magical webs for the new babies, using willow hoops and string made from plants. These dream catchers are in the shape of a circle; they filter bad dreams and allow only good dreams to enter, through a small hole in the centre of the dream catcher. When, in the morning, the first rays of sunlight hit the dream catcher, the bad dreams evaporate.

1 Begin by photocopying the dream-catcher mandala on page 385 and enlarging it. Then gather together the colouring materials you would like to use. Take a few minutes to relax and meditate on your breath.

2 Start colouring the mandala, working from the periphery toward the centre. As you colour, ask Spider Woman to filter your dreams and keep any negativity from entering. However, if there are dreams that she feels are important, and from which you need to learn something – even if they are negative – ask her to let them enter your dreaming mind.

3 When you reach the mandala's centre, ask Spider Woman to let positive dreams enter your dreamtime. Ask for dreams that will provide guidance in your daily life.

4 When you have finished your dream-catcher mandala, hang it over your bed so that the sun will hit it in the morning.

241

How to create your own mandalas

The mandala as a symbol of psychological wholeness

Swiss psychologist Carl Jung was a pioneer in the study of the human unconscious. He theorized that the unconscious was a storehouse of universal themes and images, which he called 'archetypes'.

According to Jung, the same themes and images – birth, death, parent, child, marriage, betrayal – could be found in dreams, myths, folk beliefs and religious symbols all over the world, in every era and every culture. He called the universal depository of unconscious material that was common to all humanity the 'collective unconscious'.

Jung's work with mandalas

During the 1940s Jung began to study the mandala, which he regarded as a universal archetype. Over many years he discovered that working with mandalas had a profound healing effect. Drawing and colouring mandalas helped him to bypass rational thought and gain access to the images and energy of his unconscious mind. For him, the journey to the

centre of the mandala was a symbol of the human quest for the Self – the drive to become what we truly are. Christians call this Self the soul; Tibetans call it Buddha-nature. Jung felt that, as he connected more and more with his centre – his true Self – he unleashed his energy for living.

He postulated that everything in the mandala circle outside the central point was also part of him: all the warring aspects of his personality, as well as the universal archetypes of the collective unconscious. The mandala was his whole person – his unconscious past, full of memories both acknowledged and repressed, his present life struggles and his drive to develop the future potential of his authentic Self. By drawing and colouring mandalas over time, Jung and his patients worked through issues to discover wholeness and integration – a healing that was difficult to achieve through traditional psychotherapy, which relies on verbal expression.

As Jung discovered, creating your own mandalas can help you bypass the whirl of everyday thought and use your intuition to solve problems, answer questions about your roles and identity, and gain access to insights about where you are now and where you are going.

A page from The Red Book *by psychologist Carl Jung, which documents his personal journey with mandalas.*

Tools and techniques for making mandalas

Your mandala can be entirely symmetrical or abstract and free form, and filled with symbols and images that you either draw or collage. How you create your mandala is entirely up to you.

In addition to the art supplies that are listed on page 59, there are a number of tools that can enhance your mandala-making:

• Protractor
• Double protractor
• Ruler
• See-through grid ruler
• See-through triangle
• Compass for drawing a circle
• Pencil sharpener
• Erasers
• Eraser template for precise erasing
• Scissors
• French curves
• Different-shaped templates

The mandala-making process

If you don't have a compass, use a dinner plate to create a circle. If you want a larger mandala, tie a length of string half the width of your chosen

mandala to a pen or pencil. Firmly hold down or pin the loose end of the string at the centre of your drawing surface, and then rotate the drawing instrument 360 degrees around the periphery (if your mandala is very large, you may need a friend to help with this). Experiment with using different papers and other drawing or painting surfaces that appeal to you.

Consider making tiny mandalas in a notebook, or large-scale mandalas on big pieces of paper or canvas. If you love nature, think about creating a mandala on a beach, using a stick to draw in the sand. Or you can build a more permanent large-scale mandala in your yard or garden with flowers, plants and stones. Sand mandalas (see pages 238–239) are ancient forms of mandala-making in the Native American and Tibetan

Buddhist traditions. In this part of the book you will learn to colour your own sand and make your own sand mandala (see pages 300–301).

This mandala, made of clothes and bark chips, was created in 2006 by participants at a Bioneers conference in Montana, USA.

Certain shapes (see pages 248–255) or symbols (see pages 268–277) may appear in your mandala, including birds, animals or flowers. These forms or symbols, often arising from your unconscious, provide rich material for exploration and contemplation. Understanding the meaning of these elements will help you better comprehend the meaning of your mandala. And appreciating the significance of the number of segments or parts of your mandala, or the appearance of numbers (see pages 256–267), will help you access its deeper meanings.

The five shapes and their meanings

There are five basic shapes that may emerge when you create your own mandalas. They are the circle, the equidistant cross, the spiral, the triangle and the square.

The circle

This shape represents the origin of the universe, the universe itself and the building blocks of the universe, such as the atom and the cell. As humankind's primary symbol for unity, the circle represents wholeness and completeness and stands for the psychological process of individuation, or integration. It also represents spiritual knowledge and development. The circle symbol is universal, sacred and divine. It represents the infinite nature of energy and the inclusivity of the universe – you are a part of the universe, just as it is a part of you.

Psychologist Carl Jung viewed the circle as an archetype of the psyche and the square as the archetype of the body. When combined, they symbolize the balance between psyche and body. When any symbol is shown with a circle around it, the circle invites the viewer inside it, to experience the message of the symbol. For instance, when a cross is depicted with a circle around it, the circle invites the viewer to step inside and experience the sacredness signified by the cross.

The equidistant cross

This shape represents relationship, coupling, synthesis, integration and balance. It suggests a need for connection – to a creative project, a group, another person or yourself. The equal-armed cross also symbolizes a desire to explore the deeper meaning of life. It represents a guide for your spiritual journey, and a reminder to remain authentic and true to yourself in your quest. If the equidistant cross appears in your mandala, it may suggest a deep desire to feel a part of something larger than yourself, and to feel at one with others, yourself, nature or the divine.

The spiral

This represents growth and evolution. It symbolizes the process of coming back around to something, but realizing you are at a different level, or in a different place, when you do. Spirals (see also pages 44–45) also represent the cycle of birth and death,

The circle represents wholeness and completeness and stands for the psychological process of individuation.

beginnings and ends, and the process of rebirth. They symbolize evolution and growth, as well as letting go of control, surrendering and releasing, dreams and intuition. As a spiritual symbol, the spiral represents the path from practical, ordinary, everyday consciousness to a deeper, more expansive and more intuitive understanding of reality. Spirals represent the movements between the inner and the outer worlds. In your mandala the spiral may suggest a strong need for personal or spiritual growth, as well as a need to let go of rigid ideas and ways of being.

The triangle

Bringing to mind pyramids, arrowheads and sacred mountains, the triangle represents activity, goals, visions, dreams and creative energy, as well as the integration of the masculine and feminine energies. As demonstrated in the Hindu tradition, and quite specifically in the Shri Yantra (see pages 166–173), when the triangle tips downward it symbolizes feminine energy, and when it points upward it represents masculine energy. The integrating of masculine

and feminine energies is a precursor to spiritual realizations and wholeness.

The triangle, as a representative of the number three (see pages 259–260), is associated with the process of creation. Out of the tension of opposites a third and new reality is born. In the psychological and spiritual realm, balancing thought and emotion can lead to higher wisdom. When a triangle shows up in your mandala, it suggests a need to be aware of your innate gifts, and how you integrate your masculine and feminine energies. It may suggest that you need to break through your ordinary routines and follow your dreams.

The square

This shape suggests stability, solidity, security, moral uprightness and dependability. It is made up of straight lines, which suggests something solid, fixed and immutable. The square symbolizes the ground plan or foundation of a home or other

The spiral represents the cycle of birth and death, beginnings and endings and the process of rebirth.

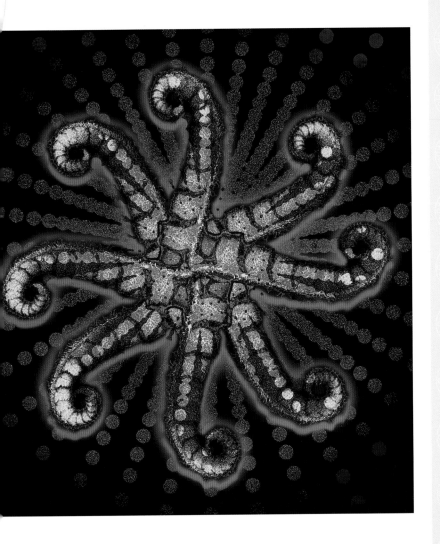

building. It is a symbol of the earth, of matter and of the material world. Its four sides also symbolize the natural, structured order of the universe as represented by the four directions (north, south, east, west) and the four seasons (winter, spring, summer, autumn). To the Ancients, the square symbolized honest business transactions, high morality and virtue. Today we refer to a 'square deal' as an honest deal. And having three 'square meals' a day relates to having three solid, balanced meals.

In Chinese belief, the square is a symbol of Earth, while the circle is representative of the heavens. When a square appears in your mandala, you are involved in constructing a foundation for your life. You are ready to build something new, to implement a plan or manifest your ideas.

In her book *Signs of Life* the cultural anthropologist and Jungian psychologist Angeles Arrien developed a test to help you further understand the meaning of the five shapes when they appear in your mandalas, and how they relate to who you are at this moment in your life. Before reading the rest of this section, quickly rank

the five shapes using a scale of one to five – with one being the shape you most favour, and five, the one that you least favour. When you are ready, read the following summary (based on Arrien's system) of the meaning of your rankings:

Position 1 represents where you believe you are. The shape placed here describes how you identify

A beautiful Tibetan Buddhist mandala, the Mandala of Compassion, Paris, Ile de France, France.

to feel safe and secure in the world, but what you really need is to find that safety, security and confidence within yourself.

Position 2 represents your strengths. The shape you have chosen as your second preference exhibits an inherent strength that is predominant in you at this time, whether or not you know it. According to Arrien, others will see this strength in you, even if you do not. The shape in this position represents an area of your life where you are comfortable and accomplished. For instance, if you chose the circle, your spiritual life may be deep and developed, but you may take this inherent strength for granted.

Position 3 represents where you really are at this time. This shape stands for the psychological and spiritual work that is under way in you at this moment. This process may be operating in your unconscious, but you must become aware of it in order to fully manifest its potential. For example, if your third shape is

yourself. It's your most familiar and most comfortable sense of yourself. However, according to Arrien, the shape in position 1 only shows where you *think* you are, or perhaps where you would *like* to be. You admire what it represents, but it may not really be you. For example, if you chose the cross for this position, you may long for a relationship in order

When a triangle shows up in your mandala, it may suggest a need to acknowledge your innate gifts.

the square, you may be starting over after a divorce. But you must be *aware* that you are creating a new foundation for your life, so that you can consciously manifest what you want, going forward.

Position 4 represents your *motivation* for what you are doing at this point in your life, which is signified by the shape in position 3. Your motivation

may be driven by past physical, mental and emotional pain that you would like to leave behind. For instance, if you are working to improve the foundations of your life – your health, your financial resources, your self-esteem – as represented by the square in position 3, then you may have arrived here because of past difficulties in your childhood or adult life.

Position 5 represents old, unfinished business. According to Arrien, this shape identifies a process or identity that you have outgrown, and that now makes you uncomfortable. For example, you may need to end an old relationship that no longer serves you. Or it could represent unresolved issues that you know you must come to terms with, but are not ready to deal with at this moment. For example, if your fifth and least-liked shape is the spiral, you may be having difficulty dealing with the death of a loved one.

When you create your mandalas, the five primary shapes (with the exception of the circle) may not appear in them. But if they do, this guide will give you an additional method of interpreting your mandalas.

Colours, shapes, symbols and
numbers all carry with them a
symbolic and archetypal resonance.
Studying their meanings will provide
you with the tools to understand your
personal mandalas on a deeper level.

*This Tibetan Buddhist mandala is
dedicated to Vajrasattva, a deity who helps
to purify negative thoughts and actions.*

255

Numbers

Sometimes random lines in your mandala may actually resemble numbers. More often, though, numbers appear in mandalas as forms or symbols.

For example, you can count the number of shapes or forms you have drawn, or the number of segments in your mandala, in order to analyse the presence of numbers in your mandala. You can even count the number of spots or drips of paint in a certain segment, or the number of lines in your entire mandala. When analysing your mandala, everything becomes meaningful and can provide tremendous insight into what is going on in your unconscious at this moment.

Below are the suggested meanings for a range of numbers from one to 13. They are not etched in stone, and you may decide that your own interpretations are more meaningful.

One

This number reflects new beginnings, or perhaps the start of a new journey. It indicates the excitement of a fresh venture, and the promise of things to come. In a metaphysical sense, the number one emerges from nothing, from the primordial void, like the *bindu* in the Hindu mandala. When the number one symbolically appears in your mandala – perhaps as the actual number one, or as a single flower or shape by itself – ask yourself what it is that you are trying to create completely anew. What is it that needs to be born in your life, and how will you recognize it when it arrives? Perhaps you need a new relationship with someone who will ignite new beginnings in your romantic or work life, or you need to do something to set your life in a fresh direction, such as take a class or move to a new apartment.

The number one appearing in your mandala may suggest a need for more focus and concentration in your life.

Alternatively, the number one can indicate completion of a past phase of your life. As a relationship or job ends, space is freed for a new person or opportunity. If your mandala is without shapes or symbols, and is filled with only one luminous colour, you may be experiencing a kind of transpersonal state of oneness with the universe. Finally, the number one may suggest the need for single-minded focus and concentration. It is only through focus and concentration that you are able to accomplish anything. When mind, body and spirit work as one, there is no end to your potential.

Two

The number two represents kindness and equality, and is the number of lovers. It also symbolizes other kinds of partnerships – business, friendship or even doctor/patient – and the act of communication. Two represents balance, such as that symbolized by an evenly weighted scale. The perfect symbol for number two is the Yin/Yang

The number two appearing in your mandala may predict a new friend, lover or business partnership.

symbol (see page 13). Here two distinct opposites move harmoniously within a circle, while each still maintains its own identity; the small opposite-coloured dot in each half symbolizes that each one contains the essence of the other.

Besides harmony, the number two can indicate strife and discord in a relationship. In a marriage, opposites can attract, and over time differences may serve to complement rather than cause problems. Two might indicate two parts of yourself: the person that you put forth to the world, and your shadow side, which is hidden. The shadow is that which you reject about yourself, or fail to recognize or acknowledge. If two identical objects appear in your mandala, consider that one may represent your shadow.

Three

The number three represents energy and motion. It suggests personal expression, and creativity. Three is the outcome of the duality in the number two, which is the creation of something new. Three can signify a family of two adults and a child. The appearance of the number three in your mandala may signal a move toward independence – from your family or your origins, from a current relationship or from a job that you have outgrown. It can also signify independent thinking.

The number three also has associations with the sacred, such as the Holy Trinity or the Triple Goddess of ancient myth (see pages 30–31). Three symbolizes completion, such as a story that has a beginning, a middle and an end. It also signifies time, as in past, present and future.

Four

Like the square, the number four represents the earth, stability, balance and foundations. The year is divided into four seasons. There are four cardinal directions: north, south, east and west. There are four basic elements: earth, air, fire and water. Fours appear in sacred architecture: Buddhist and Hindu temples are enclosed by a square with four gates. The Native American medicine wheel is divided into four quadrants, which represent the four directions. The Buddha's main teaching was the 'Four Noble Truths'.

Fours represent solidity, calmness and home. According to Carl Jung, the Ego has four fundamental ways of perceiving and interpreting reality: Thinking, Feeling, Sensation and Intuition. If you construct a mandala that contains a square or a pattern of fours, you may be in need of harmony and stability in your life.

Five

The number five represents travel and adventure. When fives appear in your mandala you may be ready for a journey. It could mean travel to another city or another country, or a spiritual journey that causes you to perceive the world differently. Five occurs in nature: the starfish has five segments; humans have a trunk, four limbs and a head, which adds up to the number five; and, of course, we have five fingers and five toes. So, five can be a symbol of the physical body. The number five in your mandala may represent your mission to contribute to the world and your desire to realize your goals.

If the number five appears in your mandala, it can suggest a personal or spiritual transformation.

Six

This number represents the union of opposites, which results in wholeness. In Greek philosophy the number six can be created with multiples of the number two (which they considered feminine) or the number three (which they considered masculine). Therefore, for the ancient Greeks the number six symbolized the sexual union of the masculine and feminine. And six-pointed stars are constructed with intersecting upward- (masculine) and downward-facing (feminine) triangles.

The number six in your mandala may represent a desire for a balanced and fulfilling relationship with the opposite sex. Or it may symbolize your desire to give birth to a painting, a novel or a piece of music. If a six shows up in your mandala, you may try working to better integrate your masculine and feminine energies. Or you may be about to meet the man or woman of your dreams.

Seven

Sevens are about mystery and esoteric meaning. In the Native American tradition there are seven directions: the four cardinal directions, plus up, down and centre. There are also seven grandfathers who represent seven virtues. In the Judeo-Christian tradition, God ended his work of creation on the seventh day. There are seven deadly sins and the seven sorrows of Mary. And there are traditionally seven virtues: Chastity, Moderation, Liberality, Charity, Meekness, Zeal and Humility.

If the number eight appears in your mandala, you may be longing for a sense of wholeness.

Eight

The number eight represents rebirth and resurrection. In the Christian tradition Christ was thought to have arisen from his grave on the eighth day after his entrance into Jerusalem. The Buddhist tradition teaches the Buddha's Eightfold Path to enlightenment. And the number eight is generally considered to be an auspicious number by numerologists. The square of any odd number, less one, is always a multiple of 8. For example, $9-1 = 8$, $25-1 = 8 \times 3$, $49-1 = 8 \times 6$, and so on.

In Babylonian mythology there were seven spheres, plus an eighth realm comprising the fixed stars, where the gods dwelled. And because of its special mathematical properties, the number eight can be a symbol of paradise. For example, Muslims believe that there are seven hells, but eight paradises. And in Jungian psychology, eight is considered a symbol of wholeness because it is a multiple of the number four, the

Correspondingly, there are seven deadly sins and seven holy sacraments.

In Buddhism there are seven stages of enlightenment. In the Hindu tradition there are seven chakras, and in Japanese mythology there are seven Lucky Gods. When seven appears in your mandala you may be attracted to ancient mystical wisdom practices or engaged in the study of those traditions.

number that represents the self. If eight appears in your mandala, you may be longing for a sense of wholeness. Or you may be experiencing a rebirth after a long, dark period of emotional pain and suffering.

Nine

Nine is a sacred number. Three times three is said to represent eternity, completion and fulfilment. And nine, as the highest single digit, symbolizes completeness. The number nine also represents the Holy Spirit and other benevolent spiritual energies. Nine is the Trinity times three. In China, nine is the number of celestial power, and the nine-storeyed pagoda is a symbol of Heaven. The Baha'i faith, which considers itself a synthesis of all religions, uses a nine-pointed star as its symbol and builds nine-sided temples.

If nine appears in your mandala, it may suggest the need for synthesis in your life, perhaps a need to bring together disparate parts of your reality into one whole. Nine may remind you that you need to bring into balance the physical, mental and spiritual aspects of your being.

Ten

Ten is said to represent perfection. Reflecting the number of our fingers, the number ten is the foundation of most counting systems, including the decimal system. In the Judeo-Christian tradition there are Ten Commandments. In the Jewish tradition it takes ten elders to convene a religious service. There are ten *sephiroth*, or divine attributes of the Tree of Life, in the Kabbalistic Jewish tradition.

If ten appears in your mandala, you may be struggling with resistance or strict adherence to a moral code. Or it may represent ten older people (teachers, relatives or friends) who are there to support you and help you with moral guidance. Tens are also strong representations of recycling events – of things coming full circle.

Eleven

The number 11 represents a metaphorical gateway, through which we integrate the inherent duality that

If the number nine appears in your mandala, you may be experiencing a need for fulfillment or completion.

is present in nature. As the ancient-wisdom traditions teach, there is enlightenment within the centre of perceived opposition. There is also wisdom in being able to tolerate paradox, in allowing two opposing ideas or truths to exist simultaneously.

The number 11 can also be a symbol of conflict, as it reflects the breakdown of the perfection of the number ten. Consequently, it can represent danger and confusion. When you bring opposing aspects of yourself into consciousness – for

If the number twelve appears in your mandala, you may need to pay attention to your use of time.

266

example, your public, professional persona and your private, chaotic, personal reality – there is bound to be a painful process of transformation. When the number 11 appears in your mandala, you may be in the throes of transition and passing through the doorway of the 11 to discover who you really are.

Twelve

The number 12 is strongly associated with cosmic order: the 12 months, the 12 signs of the Zodiac. There are 24 (= 2 x 12) hours in the day, of which 12 are daytime and the other 12 are night-time. In Greek mythology there were 12 gods and goddesses on Mount Olympus, without their leader Zeus. And the Greek hero Heracles had to spend 12 years atoning for murdering his loved ones, during which time he had to perform 12 extremely difficult tasks. These 12 tasks were eventually related to the signs of the zodiac. Jung associated the 12 labours with the hard work of individuation and with wholeness.

If the number 12 appears in your mandala you may be completing a cycle, finishing a project or ending a relationship. Or you may be experiencing a sense of wholeness as you continue your journey of growth.

Thirteen

Fear of the number 13 may relate to Judas Iscariot having been the 13th person to arrive at the Last Supper. Or it may stem from the idea that 13 spoils the wholeness and completion of the number 12. That said, there are 13 lunar months in the year, which led the Maya and the Jews to consider 13 an auspicious number. A witch's coven is composed of 13. And the first Christians numbered 13: Christ and his 12 apostles.

Thirteen, being one more than 12, points to a beginning of a new cycle. Or perhaps it denotes the ending of the last cycle. This confusion over beginnings and endings may be a source of the idea that 13 is unlucky. If this number appears in your mandala, it may be a clue that something is coming to an end at the same time as something new is starting. You may experience this as a powerful transition period, which may result in a freeing of your energy for the next phase in your life.

Symbols

Symbol-making is a deep-seated human trait that can be traced back to the hunter-gatherer era.

Consider an image of a lion. Upon seeing the lion image, you may associate it with qualities such as courage, fearlessness, strength, royalty and power. The lion now becomes more than just a picture of an animal – it is a symbol that communicates a range of meanings and qualities. As guardian figures outside a palace, a pair of lion statues may symbolize superior military prowess and communicate that unlawful entry will be met with devastating attack. As you can see, a simple image of a lion can become a series of ideas joined together: the lion plus its many associations is now a symbol.

Divine symbols

The Greek gods, each with their own distinctive forms and personalities, were not anthropomorphic, but rather, were symbols of a single divine being whose true nature is not even comprehensible by humans. The gods therefore functioned as symbols of qualities of the divine, filtered through a human lens. An image of the Buddha is filled with symbols that communicate aspects of his enlightened nature. Those who are knowledgeable about such symbols and their meanings can look at his image and gain a deeper insight into the human potential for enlightenment. Similarly, when Christ wears a crown – as Christ the King – Christians understand that His dominion over all creatures is an essential part of His nature and not one acquired by violence. His crown does not symbolize human power, but rather the act of loving and serving others.

These divine figures and images are human attempts to symbolize the ineffable – that which is too great to be expressed in words. They also present the surface of that which is hidden and veiled, which may require deeper exploration. Symbols challenge

Christ's crown symbolizes His Kingship, which is not based on human power but on loving and serving others.

you to go beyond the surface to discover complex ideas and concepts and rich, expansive layers of meaning.

When you create your own mandalas, you may find yourself drawing images that symbolize deeper layers of yourself, and some of the symbols that may be contained within them are explained on the following pages.

The meaning of symbols in your mandalas

As we have seen, mandalas are a tool for connecting with that which is greater than yourself – God, your higher self, your inner self or the 'source'. The symbols that may appear in them are many and various.

Here is a sampling of a few common symbols and their historical meanings. You can look up the significance of other images and symbols that may appear in your mandalas in reference books or online. However, there is no one definitive meaning of a symbol, and only you can decide what significance an image actually has for you.

Cat

The cats is an inscrutable, nocturnal creature. The ancient Egyptians and the early Christians revered it. Unfortunately, cats were persecuted as the 'familiars' (attending spirits) of so-called witches during the Middle Ages and became anathema to the Church at that time. Cats symbolize independence, and the merging of the spiritual with the physical and of the psychic with the sensual. They also represent wisdom, and manifest confidence and self-assurance when confronted. They reach the height of their powers at night and are associated with the moon. A cat image in your mandala may symbolize your growing independence; or it could be your own cat, in the form of a 'familiar' or 'attending spirit'.

Dog

The dog, an emblem of faithfulness and guardianship, has been one of the most widely kept working and companion animals in human history. Dogs embody courage, playfulness, sociability and intelligence, and possess excellent hunting skills. In 13th-century France a greyhound was revered as a saint – St Guinefort. The Greco-Romans, who described those from elsewhere as 'dog-headed' peoples, depicted St Christopher, who was from the tribe of the Marmaritae, with the head of a dog. In your mandala this symbol may represent your own dog or positive canine qualities, such as courage, loyalty or playfulness, that you possess or would like to possess.

Mouse

In ancient Greece and Rome, mice symbolized negative qualities such as avarice, greed and thievery, because of their destruction of grain stores. In Buddhist lore the deity Ganesha rides a mouse, as a symbol of intelligence and the ability to penetrate all obstacles. In Africa, diviners use mice to determine fortunes. Because mice live so close to the ground, they are believed to have an intimate relationship with Earth spirits and ancestors. If a mouse appears in your mandala it may represent your hidden or unrecognized intelligence.

Bee

In many cultures bees have been thought of as messengers of the spirits. In Celtic lore they represent the wisdom of the Otherworld. In ancient Egypt bees represented the soul and, when carved on tombs, symbolized immortality. On ancient Greek coins from the city of Ephesus a queen bee appears as a symbol of the Great Mother. And the Roman god of love, Cupid, is often pictured with bees or being stung. During the medieval period monasteries were centres of bee-keeping, and so in Christianity the bee came to symbolize industry, fidelity and virginity. A bee in your mandala may represent a message from a guardian spirit.

Butterfly

For Christians, the butterfly's three steps of metamorphosis – from caterpillar, to pupa, to winged insect – symbolize spiritual transformation. For the Aztec and Maya, the butterfly was the symbol of the god of fire, Xiutecutli, and fire transformed both food and metal. For Native American tribes from the Canadian north-west, the butterfly is associated with the trickster because of its unpredictable flight. In all cultures, because the butterfly is so fragile, it symbolizes human frailty; and because of its short life it is also a symbol of the ephemeral nature of physical existence. Butterflies in your mandala may mean that you are in transition from one phase of your life to the next, or that you are finally coming into your own.

Owl

The owl symbolizes wisdom, intelligence, mystery, mysticism and secrets. In ancient cultures it was considered the ruler of the night, guardian of the Underworlds and protector of the dead. In ancient Greece the owl was sacred to the goddess Athena. Because of its ability to see at night, the owl was invoked by Native Americans as an oracle of hidden knowledge. In Europe, during medieval times, owls were considered witches and wizards in disguise. And in Indian culture a white owl is a companion of Lakshmi, the goddess of wealth. An owl appearing in your mandala may indicate knowledge that you are hiding from yourself.

Octopus

The octopus symbolizes mystery, flexibility, fluidity, intelligence, adaptability and unpredictability. It is a lunar creature that is affected by the tides and the waxing and waning of the moon. It dwells on the ever-changing, shifting bottom of the ocean and, not having a skeleton, it can move quickly and escape with ease from the tightest of places. It even has the capability to detach a limb in order to escape from a predator. The appearance of an octopus in your mandala symbolizes a heightening of creativity, a movement toward goals in unorthodox ways and the ability to lose excess emotional or physical baggage.

In many cultures the owl represents mystery, secrets, wisdom and hidden knowledge.

Snake

The snake trying to swallow its tail is a symbol for eternity and life begetting life. One of the most complex symbols in the world, it represents both male and female, death and destruction, life and resurrection, light and darkness, good and evil, healing and poison, and wisdom and blind passion. Because the snake sheds its skin, it symbolizes letting go of the past and rebirth. It lives in the Underworld or realm of the dead, and represents both the unconscious and transcendence. As a phallic symbol, it represents sexuality and sexual union. If a snake appears in your mandala, you may be letting go of an old relationship or way of being.

Frog

In folklore frogs are depicted as powerless and ugly, but brimming with hidden, undeveloped talents. Because they lay enormous quantities of eggs, they symbolize fertility and abundance. In Egypt, Heket was the frog-headed goddess of birthing. In Christianity the frog's three stages of development – egg, tadpole and adult amphibian – symbolize spiritual

evolution. In Christian art, the frog is a symbol of the Holy Trinity. For the Celtic people the frog represented healing. And in China the frog is an emblem of good luck. If a frog appears in your mandala, you may need to acknowledge your talents.

In mythology, the frog represents hidden talents, fertility, abundance and spiritual evolution.

Rose

For the ancient Greeks and Romans the rose symbolized love and beauty, as well as the goddesses of love, Aphrodite and Venus. Aphrodite gave a rose to her son Eros, the god of love, who in turn gave it to Harpocrates, the god of silence, to make certain that his mother's indiscretions remained secret. In ancient Rome a rose would be placed on the door of a room where confidential matters were being discussed. The phrase *sub rosa*, or 'under the rose', means to keep a secret and is derived from this practice; in Christianity, this phrase was associated with confession, and roses were often carved on confessionals, indicating that the priest would maintain secrecy. The red rose eventually became a symbol of the blood of the Christian martyrs and of the Virgin Mary. A rose in your mandala may mean that you are finally recognizing your beauty.

Oak tree

In Celtic mythology the oak represents doors and gateways between worlds, or marks the place where portals to the Underworld could be erected. In Norse mythology the oak was sacred to the thunder god, Thor, possibly because oaks – being the largest tree in northern Europe – often drew lightning in a storm. In Greek mythology the oak was a symbol of Zeus and his sacred tree. The oracle of Dodona, in prehistoric north-western Greece, consisted solely of a holy oak, and priestesses and priests interpreted the rustling of its leaves to determine the correct actions to be taken. If a tree appears in your mandala, you may be accessing a deeper part of your psyche.

The oak tree represents a gateway to hidden worlds and the deeper parts of the psyche.

Spider

The spider symbolizes mystery, power, growth, the feminine, death and rebirth, resourcefulness and fate. Most spiders have eight eyes, and all have eight legs, the number eight being a symbol of infinity. In Greek mythology, Arachne was a gifted weaver whom Athena challenged to a duel – but no one could confirm the victor. Arachne was arrogant, so Athena punished her; Arachne took this hard and killed herself. In remorse, Athena resurrected Arachne in the form of a spider so that she would forever be the best weaver of the universe. If a spider appears in your mandala, she is there to protect you from bad dreams.

Archetypes

Carl Jung, the Swiss psychiatrist and founder of analytical psychology, believed that symbol creation was a key to understanding human nature. He understood symbols to be an expression of something that is essentially difficult to explain or know.

He investigated the symbols of different religious, mythological and magical systems in many cultures and time periods, and discovered remarkable similarities. To account for these, he suggested that the unconscious is divided into two layers.

The personal and collective unconscious

The first layer he called the 'personal unconscious' – the reservoir of material acquired by an individual through his or her life, which he or she has mostly forgotten or repressed. The second layer he named the 'collective unconscious', which contains the cellular memories that are common to all humankind. These common memories and experiences form archetypes – or primordial, symbolic images that reflect basic patterns and universal themes common to all peoples. Examples of archetypes are the Shadow, the Old Wise Person, the Trickster, the Mother, the Father, the Orphan and the Innocent Child. There are also nature archetypes that are common to all people, such as fire, ocean, river, mountain, sky and tree, as well as animals, birds and insects.

Jung discovered that, because of the collective unconscious, humans have a disposition to react to life in a similar way to human beings who have gone before. He uncovered patterns that are distinctly human that structure our minds and imagination. For example, the Old Wise Person may appear in the mandalas of three different people: as a grandmother in one, as an old beggar on the street in another and as a priest or rabbi in a third. A dove will have a different effect on the unconscious mind than a black cat. Archetypes and archetypal images appear in novels, movies, music and plays. The *Harry Potter* novels are filled with archetypal images, which partly explain their unprecedented worldwide popularity. Jung postulated that, as human beings, we share in a single Universal Unconscious which is called the 'collective unconscious', and even our personal unconscious is shaped according to universal patterns.

The hot flames of fire, which embody the power and essence of the Universe, are a symbol of creation.

279

Exercise The ten-minute mandala

Creating a small mandala, in the evening before bed, is a good way to 'check in' with yourself and see where you are – physically, emotionally, mentally and spiritually.

This ten-minute mandala provides a quick way of bringing to consciousness all the loose ends of the day. If you have vague feelings of dissatisfaction, or niggling worries that are not quite formulated, creating a small mandala will not only help you quell any anxieties, but will also sort out your feelings in a nurturing and constructive way. The ten-minute mandala can also help you process the various experiences of the past day – at work, at home, with your partner or friends – so that you can get a good night's rest.

Alternatively, it can be a wonderful morning exercise. Taking just ten minutes to create a beautiful miniature mandala sets a positive tone for the day ahead. If you have any anxieties about work, the act of drawing and colouring will calm your nerves. Starting your morning with an act of creativity can establish your

intention for this creativity to manifest throughout the rest of your day.

This is a small mandala – ideally just 7.5 cm (3 in) in diameter – that you can complete in ten minutes (or less). When you create a mandala in this way, you not only get a good idea of where you are in this moment, but also, a glimpse of where you are in the larger macro-trajectory of your life. The phrase 'start where you are' means accepting yourself wherever you are right now (morning or evening) and moving on from there. Whatever you are feeling, thinking or yearning for at this moment is okay.

1 Choose the art supplies you would like to use to create your mandala. It is best to work with dry media, such as coloured pencils, so that you have minimal preparation time. Create your ten-minute mandalas in your Mandala Journal, or in a small drawing book that you keep for this

purpose. There is no need to do this in a special place or to be alone when you are doing this exercise.

2 Create a circle on the paper, either freehand or using a compass. After you have drawn the circle, close your eyes briefly and set the intention that you will be open to and accepting of whatever emerges from the mandala.

3 Have a clock or watch in view so that you can keep track of time. If you wish, set an alarm for ten minutes. As you create your mandala, meditate on your breath. Try not to think of anything in particular. If thoughts arise, simply let them pass by. Focus on the movement of your hand and the physical act of creating the mandala. Let the feeling of drawing and colouring permeate your entire body. If your thoughts wander to what happened during your day at work, or what you anticipate for the day ahead, bring your attention back to your breath.

4 Work quickly and continuously. Let forms, symbols or colours emerge without censoring them (you only have ten minutes). If your mandala is dark and disturbing, try not to inhibit whatever

is emerging. Likewise, if it is beautiful and peaceful, try not to add emotions that may not be there at the moment.

5 After you have completed your mandala, spend a few minutes taking it in. How does it make you feel? What images or symbols (see pages 268–277) – if any – appear in it? What do the colours (see pages 60–91) tell you? Is your mandala divided into parts and, if so, what does the number symbolism (see pages 256–267) tell you?

6 Now write in your Mandala Journal, briefly, for one minute. Answer the question 'Where am I right now?' Write down in words what your ten-minute mandala is saying to you about your spiritual, emotional and psychological condition. The whole process of creating your mandala, thinking and writing about it should take no more than 15 minutes.

7 When you are finished, dedicate your mandala by generating a sense of love and acceptance for yourself as you are at this moment in time.

Exercise Free-form mandala

In this exercise you are invited to create a mandala by simply drawing and colouring what you feel like, without the use of any 'tools', such as a protractor, compass or shape-template.

The periphery of your mandala will hold and contain whatever your psyche wants to express at this moment. Here symmetry does not come into play, unless you want it to.

The shape of the mandala can be filled in any way you desire. Your drawing skills (or lack thereof) are not important at all. The most important aspect of this exercise is letting go of any self-judgment or inhibitions. If you feel playful and joyful, that is great! If you feel emotional and need to express your sadness or fear, that is really okay. If you are not feeling anything in particular, just begin.

There is no right way to do this exercise, except perhaps to start with a closed shape, which you can 'fill in' with drawing and colour. You can use a guide to draw a circle or, if you really want to be free form, simply draw a basic circle freehand. You also have the

option of creating a square mandala, like the shape of some Hindu (see pages 167–169) and Native American (see pages 234–239) sand mandalas – again with or without a guide.

1 Before you begin, assemble your materials. You will need a large sheet of drawing paper, 35 x 43 cm (14 x 17 in) or larger; colouring materials – for example, crayons, coloured pencils, chalks, markers, watercolours or acrylic paint; and a large dinner plate, frying-pan lid or other circular shape to use as a guide (unless you are drawing your circle freehand).

2 If you wish, choose pleasant instrumental music to play in the background. Find a time and place where you can be alone and undisturbed for about an hour.

3 This exercise begins with an extended breath meditation. Start by closing your

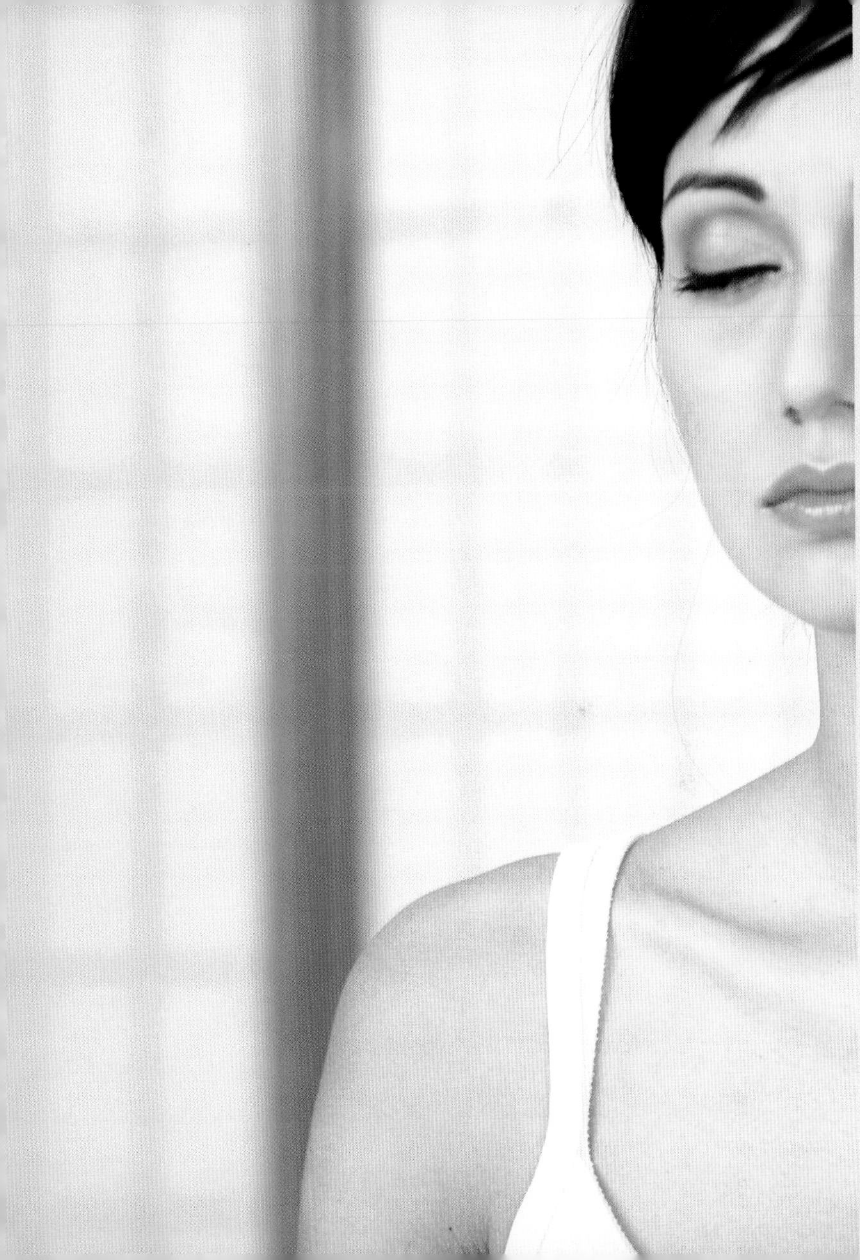

eyes. Breathe normally and naturally, and gently allow your awareness to be on your breathing. Simply observe your breath, trying not to control or alter it in any conscious way. You will find that at times your attention drifts away from your breath and you are thinking about other things or listening to noises outside. Whenever you notice that you are not observing your breath, gently bring your attention back to your breathing.

4 Practise this meditation technique for 15 minutes. At the end of that time keep your eyes closed and just sit easily for two or three minutes. Allow yourself to come out of the meditation gradually, before opening your eyes. Now you are ready to begin creating your mandala.

5 First, place your plate or other shape flat down on the paper and, with a light colour or pencil, trace around it (or draw your circle or square freehand).

6 Your task is only to fill the circle or square with whatever you feel belongs there. Fill it with those shapes, colours or images that feel right to you. There are no rules, and no guidelines. And there are no accidents – what may seem at first like a

squiggly 'mistake' might become one of several ripples on water, and so on.

7 Draw quickly, simply allowing your inner spirit to express itself on paper. Try not to censor yourself or to let any preconceived notions or 'rules' interfere. If you feel like drawing something hideous, go right ahead. Do not be concerned about your drawing abilities or about whether what you draw looks like what you intended.

8 Draw and colour until you feel the mandala is telling you to stop. It may be complete at this point, or you can set it aside and work on it again at another time.

9 Once your mandala is finished, date it. If you have worked on it over several days, write down the date of each day that it was worked on.

10 Hang your free-form mandala on the wall where you can see it regularly. Each day spend a few moments simply looking at it, and allow it to explain itself to you. Consult the sections in this book on colour (see pages 60–91), number (see pages 256–267), symbol (see pages 268–277) and shape (see pages 248–255) to help you interpret its meaning.

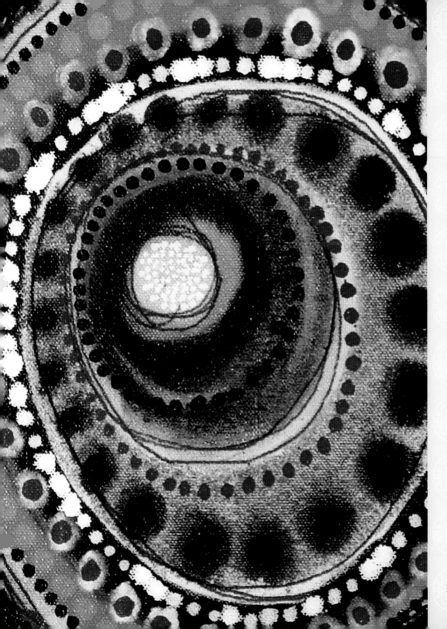

Exercise Kaleidoscope mandala

There is something very soothing and aesthetically pleasing about
a mandala that is centred and symmetrical. When completed, a
kaleidoscope mandala may look very intricate, but it is not that
complicated to create. With patience, accuracy in measuring and a
sense of colour, you are on your way to creating an exquisite mandala.

1 For this exercise you will need a heavy
sheet of drawing or watercolour paper
approximately 23 x 30 cm (9 x 12 in); a
pencil, compass, ruler and protractor; and
coloured pencils or water-based paints. Set
your compass at 9 cm (3½ in) and draw a
circle in the centre of the paper: this is the
perimeter of your kaleidoscope mandala.

2 Now you are going to divide your mandala
into 12 sections using your protractor. Place
it in the middle of the circle you have just
drawn. Line up the dot marking the middle
of the flat edge of the protractor with the
point in the centre of your circle. Hold the
protractor in position and make a pencil
dot next to the following degrees on your
protractor: 0, 30, 60, 90, 120, 150, 180.

3 Turn your protractor upside down and,
once again, centre the middle of the
protractor with the centre point of your

circle. Then line up the 0 and 180 degree
marks on the protractor with the 0 and
180 degree marks you just made before
you turned it upside down. Now, mark
the remaining degrees on your protractor:
30, 60, 90, 120, 150.

4 Now, using your ruler, draw a pencil
line from the periphery through each
dot to the centre of the circle. When you
finish your mandala should be divided
into 12 equal sections.

5 Using either coloured pencils or water-
based paints, begin by making a small
circle at the centre of your mandala with
your compass. Use this centre to begin
painting, and then work outward. As you
paint, try to maintain symmetry as you
go. Take your time and measure, when
necessary, to maintain the ordered quality
of the kaleidoscope.

Labyrinth mandalas

A labyrinth is a circular form made up of a single circuitous
path. It is an ancient symbol that represents journey, discovery
and transformation.

As a meditative tool, the labyrinth requires your active participation. You walk the path of a large labyrinth, or use your finger to trace a small version on paper. At its deepest level,

the labyrinth is both archetype (see pages 278–279) and metaphor for the journey of life, and the journey inward into your deepest self.

A labyrinth is different from a maze. A maze requires you to negotiate its many wrong turns and dead ends in order to reach the centre. In contrast, a labyrinth has only one continuous path to its centre. You leave the centre by retracing that same path out to your starting point. Also, a labyrinth is not a spiral; it has a perimeter, whereas a spiral does not. In order to better understand the labyrinth's structure it is best to imagine viewing it from above, as if looking down on the foundation of a building from the air.

The round outside perimeter has only one opening, where the path to the centre begins. The lines themselves create the 'walls' of the labyrinth, and the space between the lines form the 'path'. The path fills the entire interior space, which is made up of circuits that fold back on themselves, change

A labyrinth is a metaphor for the journey of life and the journey inward to your deepest self.

direction and bring you close to – and then away from – the centre. Each time you enter a different circuit, you turn 180 degrees. As you change direction, you shift your awareness from right-brain to left-brain, which induces more receptive states of consciousness. Eventually you reach the centre, a place for meditation, prayer or reflection. What you discover or receive while there is absorbed and integrated on your walk out.

The labyrinth as a metaphor for spiritual transformation

The labyrinth form is a beautiful metaphor for spiritual and personal transformation. The entrance of the labyrinth marks the start of a journey: one that takes you away from your normal everyday life and leads you inward. Inside, the space is very complicated and somewhat confusing. A spiritual journey – one that asks the larger questions, such as the purpose of existence, the nature of God or divinity, or the reality of good and evil – is not an easy one. It is often filled with doubt, it can be complicated and confusing, and even beginning the journey takes courage and maturity.

The path inside the labyrinth has the maximum number of twists and turns that the space can accommodate, and provides the longest route to the centre. Just as you seem to be reaching the centre, the path takes you away from it. Like the spiritual path, it is sometimes frustrating and difficult; you may feel it is not worth it, or perhaps that you are not worthy or capable. But if you can stand the anxiety and stress and don't give up, you will eventually reach the centre.

Once in the centre, you are alone with yourself, God, your higher power, or whatever or whomever you are looking for. This encounter profoundly changes you, and you understand that you cannot go back to how and what you were. You make a 180-degree turn and begin following the path back to the entrance, to a new beginning, with new spiritual realizations to carry you forward. You are not the same person who entered the labyrinth.

Walking the path of the labyrinth may be frustrating and difficult, but it is worth it when you reach the centre.

Exercise How to create a labyrinth mandala

A small labyrinth can be drawn or painted on a piece of paper and traced with your finger. Or you can draw or paint one on a large piece of canvas, for use in a big indoor space.

Large labyrinths can also be created using masking tape on a floor (for instance, in a school gym). You can also create an outdoor labyrinth using stones, bricks, candles, plants or flowers, strings of Christmas-tree lights or anything else that you favour to mark a path, either temporarily or permanently. If you have access to a beach, you can create a large labyrinth by tracing its path in the sand.

The following illustration shows you how to create a classical seven-circuit labyrinth from Crete.

1 The easiest way is to start with a cross, then add right-angles between the arms of the cross.

2 Place a dot in each right-angle, then connect them in the order shown.

3 If you add two additional right-angles you will get a larger, 11-circuit labyrinth.

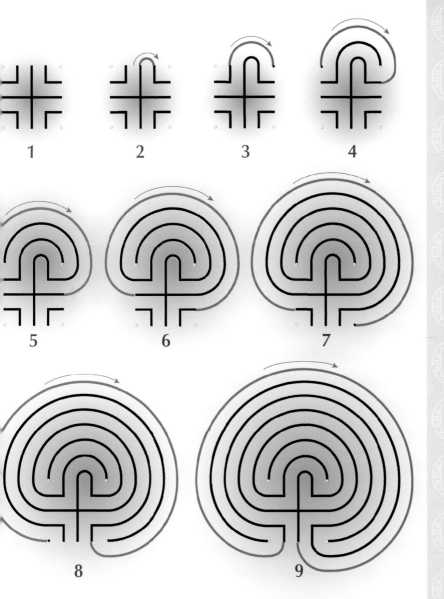

1   2   3   4

5   6   7

8   9

Exercise Labyrinth meditation for creating balance

This exercise requires you to have made a big mandala in sand on the beach, or to have painted one on a large tarpaulin or canvas (see pages 294–295). But the instructions for following the labyrinth are the same whether it is small or large.

The right side of the brain is the area of creativity and emotions, while the left side of the brain is the area of analysis and judgment. Activities that stimulate the left-brain are solving crossword puzzles, performing learning tasks, speaking and writing, analysing and problem-solving; those that stimulate the right brain are emotional issues, the creative process, seeing or feeling different sizes, perceiving colours, performing exercises involving timing, seeing unfamiliar faces and meeting someone new. The labyrinth process of turning from right to left will help you to balance your right-brain and left-brain.

1 Stand balanced on both feet, with your spine straight and your shoulders relaxed, at the entrance to the labyrinth. Close your eyes and breathe for a few minutes to calm and centre yourself.

2 Open your eyes and begin your journey into the labyrinth. On this walk try not to think of anything. When thoughts or feelings emerge, simply bring your attention to the path. Keep your head facing forward.

3 When you come to a 180-degree turn, consciously move your head and eyes in the direction that you are going, keeping them on the path ahead. When you come to the next turn, move your body, head and eyes in the opposite direction. Walk slowly and steadily, with your focus and concentration on the path and on your eye movement.

4 When you reach the centre, stand still with your eyes closed. Meditate on your breath for as long as you like. Again,

if thoughts or feelings intrude, do not entertain them. When you are ready, open your eyes and begin your journey back in the same way, slowly and carefully paying attention to the path and to your eye movement.

5 When you reach the entrance again, stand for a minute and notice whether you feel any different from the way you felt when you started.

Exercise Labyrinth meditation for increasing creativity

Labyrinth-tracing using a small labyrinth mandala can help you bypass the mental chatter of your left-brain and access your right-brain – the source of your creative expression.

1 Draw or paint a small labyrinth to use in this meditation following the instructions that are given on pages 294–295. When you have completed the labyrinth, trace the lines with liquid glue. Before the glue dries, cover the labyrinth with gold or silver glitter. Remove any excess glitter by pouring it from the paper back into the pot.

2 Place your labyrinth on a table in front of you. Close your eyes, breathe deeply to clear your mind and to prepare to enter the labyrinth.

3 Using the index finger of your non-dominant (non-writing) hand, begin to trace the path of the labyrinth slowly and deliberately toward the centre. If you have fears about 'letting go' in the creative process, or doubts about your talents or skills, witness those hindrances and inhibitions falling away.

4 With each turn feel yourself getting closer to your creative centre. This is a place where you can be uninhibited, spontaneous, joyful and playful. Your creative centre may also be the source of profound spiritual realizations.

5 When you reach the centre, place the palm of your non-dominant hand over it. Place your other palm over your heart. Close your eyes and let the energy flow between your heart and the centre of the labyrinth.

6 When you are ready, begin tracing the path from the centre back to the entrance. As you do so, meditate on the thought that you are a channel for the expression of the universe's profound joy and perennial truths.

Exercise Sand mandala

Both Tibetan Buddhists and Native Americans create mandalas out of coloured sand. In each case the mandala is deliberately designed to be impermanent. Monks and medicine men create elaborate and beautiful designs for healing and meditation and then, in each tradition, carefully brush the mandalas into a pile and return them to nature.

In this exercise you will learn how to make your own sand mandala. The sand used in traditional sand mandalas is coloured with natural dyes, although you will be using food dyes for your first sand mandala. But if working with sand appeals to you, you may wish to learn how to make your own natural dyes and colour your sand in the traditional manner.

1 First, purchase some fine white sand. You may want to buy 0.5 kg (1 lb) for a small mandala, or more for a larger one. Then, in an old food blender, mix five or six colours to start with, and store each colour in a separate jar. Alternatively, you can purchase coloured sand in a broad range of colours at craft stores.

2 On a board or heavy piece of cardboard that is about 60 cm (2 ft) square, draw the blueprint of your sand mandala. Take a moment to envision the colours of sand that you will use for each section.

3 Take apart an old pen so that you end up with a thin plastic tube. Fill the tube with your first coloured sand and, very lightly, tap the tube so that the sand begins to flow out, filling a defined area. Be patient and work slowly outward from the centre of the mandala.

4 When all sections of the blueprint are completely filled with coloured sand, your sand mandala is finished.

5 Meditate for a few minutes on change and impermanence and how these realities manifest in your life. When you are ready, complete the sand-mandala process by sweeping up your mandala and discarding it in an outdoor location in a natural setting.

Exercise A month of mandalas

In this final exercise you are invited to create a mandala
every day for one month.

One approach is to create a
variety of mandalas of different
sizes, using different materials.
For example, you could create a
mandala on a beach one day and
a small ten-minute mandala the
next. Your mandalas can be small or
large, painted on canvas or drawn on
paper, created freehand or in a more
symmetrical fashion, and with or
without images. It is up to you how
you create them. The aim is to be
engaged in the mandala-making
process on a daily basis and to
process what emerges.

Another approach is to buy a
sketchbook or a watercolour book
with at least 30 sheets. This allows
you to work on your mandalas as a
series, keeping the size and art media
for each mandala the same. In this
way the focus will be more on the
content of the mandala as it presents
itself each day. It is best to do one
mandala on each page, leaving the

reverse side of the sheet untouched.
Then you have the option of writing
on the opposite blank page about
the meaning of that particular
mandala for you. Alternatively, you
can write about your mandalas in
your Mandala Journal.

At the end of the month – using
the various guides to colour, shape,
number, symbol and archetype in this
book – review your mandalas as one
complete body of work and notice
whether any patterns emerge.

Because you cannot see directly
into your unconscious, it helps to
have a mirror so that you can observe
the dynamic forces that operate within
you. Mandala art can provide you
with just such a mirror. By drawing
and colouring mandalas you can shift
your attention from external concerns,
reconnect with your body, mind and
spirit and with your own higher self,
which aspires to live more freely and
creatively in the world.

Mandala
workbook

40 beautiful mandala illustrations for colouring and meditation

In this section you will find mandalas based on the Hindu, Buddhist, Christian, Celtic and Native American traditions. They are here for you to colour, and for inspiration. To preserve them for future use you may wish to photocopy them.

Durga yantra

The goddess Durga, the warrior aspect of the Divine Mother,
is a compassionate protector in times of danger or distress.

Bhuvanesvari yantra

The goddess Bhuvanesvari illuminates the Universe with her radiant beauty, and helps give form to nascent ideas.

Cosmic mandala

The center represents the One from which everything emanates, and the cosmic unity underlying everything in the Universe.

Kali yantra

Kali, Mother of the Universe, and goddess of creation and
destruction, gives protection and courage in times of fear.

Fourth aspect of Kali

The goddess Bhuvanesvari, the fourth aspect of Kali, embodies
the dynamic energy underlying all creative activity.

Sarvamangala Nitya

The goddess Sarvamangala, representing the thirteenth of fifteen moon mandalas, grants material and spiritual progress.

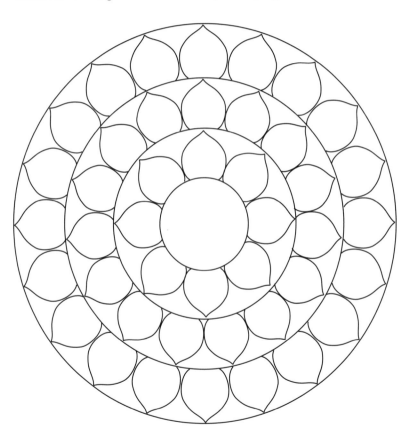

Surya yantra

Devotion to the sun god Surya strengthens willpower, builds discipline and provides courage to face the day.

Shri yantra

All creation, manifestation and dissolution are considered to be the play of the Red Goddess, Lalita Tripurasundari.

Wheel of Dharma

The Buddha's Eightfold Path requires right view, intention, speech, action, livelihood, effort, mindfulness, concentration and wisdom.

Cosmic mandala

The sun, moon and other planets orbit around Mount Meru, the Buddhist centre of the universe.

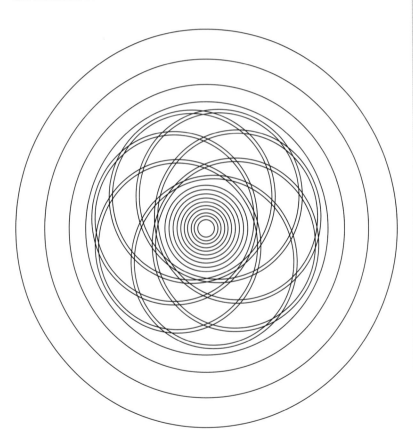

Second cosmic mandala

Buddhists understand the universe as one of many universes that will come and go through endless time.

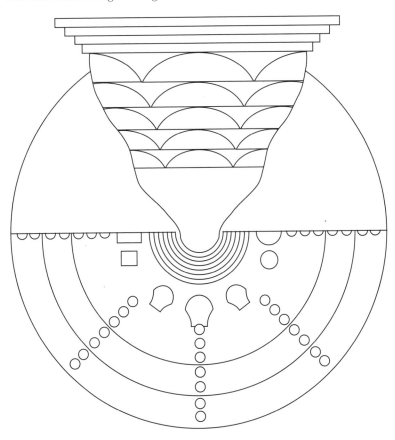

Japanese star mandala

This mandala represents the 36 guardians that protect 28 bodhisattvas – enlightened beings who vow to save all others.

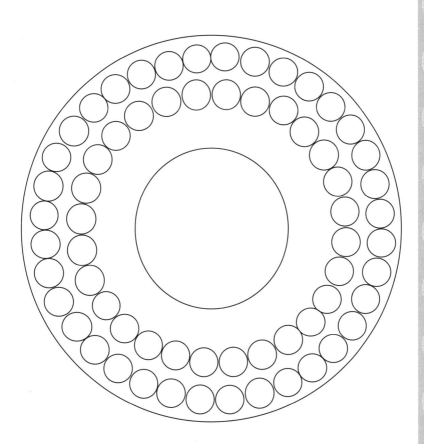

Vajrayogini

Vajrayogini, a female Buddha, represents complete mastery over ego, and the transformation of desire and attachment into enlightenment.

Wheel of Life

The Buddhist Wheel of Life helps you to look deeply into your
inner being to discover the obstacles to your enlightenment.

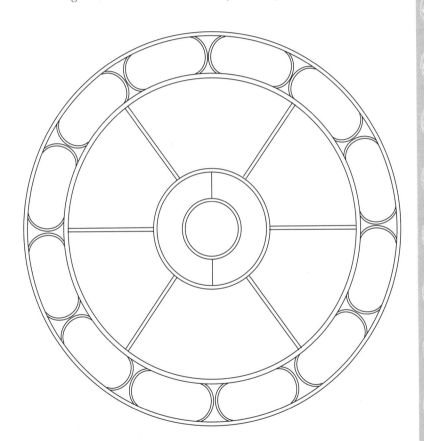

Wheel of Time

Kalachakra, the Wheel of Time, promotes worldly and inner peace and balance within the body.

Yama Chamunda mandala

Yama, Lord of Death, and his consort Chamunda protect from untimely death and rebirth in the lower realms.

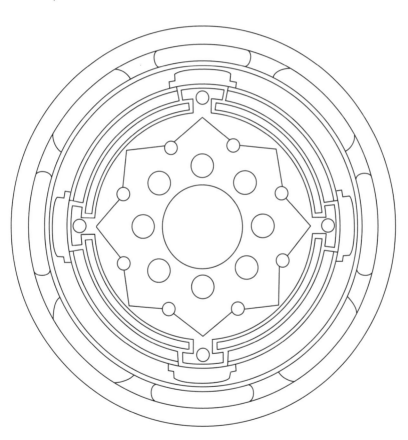

San Lorenzo, Turin

The dome in sacred architecture expresses our yearning for immortality, transcendence, God in heaven and the afterlife.

Sainte-Chapelle, Paris

The apocalypse reveals Jesus Christ as Messiah
and harkens the beginning of a new era.

East rose, Laon Cathedral

Holy Mary, Mother of God, prays for us, now and
at the hour of our death.

MANDALA WORKBOOK

West rose, Notre-Dame de Paris

Mary, the compassionate protector, the one who understands sorrows, intercedes for the faithful in their desire to approach God.

Rose window, Notre Dame en Vaux

Mary wears a crown and is seated on a throne to
show her royal descent from the House of David.

Rose window, Orvieto Cathedral

Christ is surrounded by four Doctors of the Church:
Pope Gregory the Great, Jerome, Ambrose and Augustine.

South rose, St Maurice, Angers

Christ in Majesty, seated on a throne, inspires confidence and projects towering strength as Eternal Victor and Eternal King.

South rose window, Chartres

When God became a human through his son Jesus Christ,
all existence became endowed with a sea of blessings.

Aberlemno stone

The triple spiral in contemporary Celtic paganism stands for the three realms, Land, Sea and Sky, or the Triple Goddess.

Animal interlacing

Interlaced Celtic animal forms celebrate our human interrelationship and interdependence with the animal world.

Celtic knotwork

Celtic knots symbolize the ineffable, and express a sense
of oneness with the never-ending cycle of life.

Nature spirals

As the lines of Celtic knots are interwoven, so are we interwoven with everything in nature and the Universe.

Celtic shield

Early Celtic shields were made of bronze and wood. They symbolize psychic as well as physical protection.

Interlacing snake motif

For the ancient Celts, the snake symbolized transformation and renewal, and was associated with the horned god Cernunnos.

Key pattern, Lindisfarne

Key patterns suggest a spiritual journey through a labyrinth.
They also symbolize protection.

Lindisfarne detail

The monk Eadfrith created the illuminated manuscript known as the Lindsfarne Gospels in the early 700s CE.

Bison robe sun

Bison robes were worn to protect against the elements, and decorated with symbols representing spiritual beliefs.

Four directions basket

For the Lakota, everything in this world comes from the four cardinal directions. Each direction has a sacred meaning.

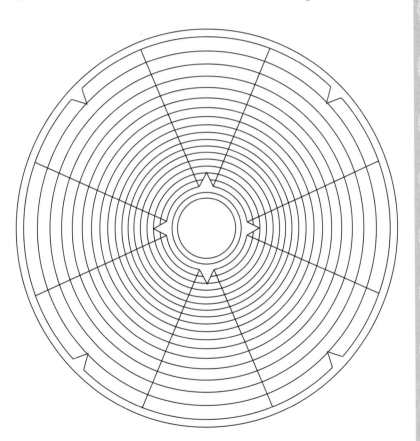

Mimbres turtle

For the ancient Mimbres peoples of the American Southwest,
the turtle symbolized ancestors and longevity.

Mimbres bowl

The Mimbres peoples of the American Southwest created distinctive pottery for use in sacred ceremonies.

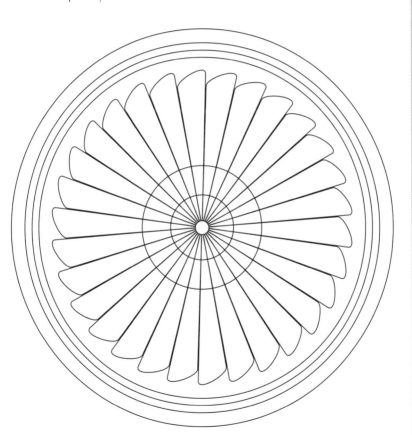

Navajo wedding basket

The line from the center to the outer rim means there is always a pathway through darkness to light.

Pima basket, Arizona

The Pima symbol for life is the maze, and at the centre
of the maze are one's dreams and goals.

Sioux beadwork

In the Sioux Universe, the sun was a primary deity,
and the sun dance, the most important ritual.

Dream catcher

The dream catcher attracts dreams to its web. Good dreams
pass through, but bad dreams will get caught.

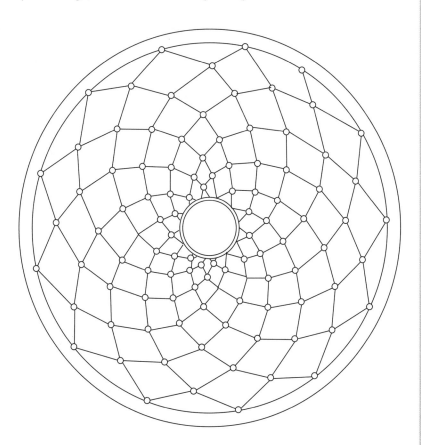

Glossary

Archetype A primordial, symbolic image that reflects basic patterns and universal themes common to all peoples.

Bindu A sacred Hindu point, the source from which everything that exists emanates.

Buddhist path This emphasizes Buddha-nature, or the potential for enlightenment.

Cardinal directions The four compass points of north, south, east and west.

Cell The essential structure of all living things.

Chakra One of seven 'wheels' or hubs of energy that are vertically aligned along the human spine, in Hindu belief.

Chi Vital energy, in Traditional Chinese Medicine.

Dream catcher A mandala-like wooden hoop, in Native American tradition, with a 9 cm (3½ in) diameter filled with a weblike net, and a feather in the centre; it is believed to attract dreams to its web.

Hindu path This is about realization of the self as one with the divine.

Karma The consequences of our actions in this life or in the next; all actions have consequences: good actions have good consequences; negative actions have negative consequences.

Mandala A sacred symbol of the spiritual journey, and a two-dimensional pictorial representation of a multi-dimensional divine universe, sometimes translated as 'essence container'; the primordial circle of existence.

Medicine wheel A large mandala in the landscape, made by Native Americans using stones and other markers.

Meridian An energy pathway, in Traditional Chinese Medicine, carrying 'chi' or vital energy through the body.

Nirvana The first step of spiritual liberation, in Buddhist belief.

Petroglyph Spirals and other images incised in stone, on cliffs, boulders and cave walls.

Prana Vital energy, in the Hindu tradition.

Samsara The world of suffering and eternal reincarnation, in the Hindu and Buddhist traditions.

Sand mandala In the Navajo tradition, this depicts Holy People acting in the sacred world and is created by sprinkling fine grains of coloured sand on top of a smooth bed of fine sand; the sand mandala is the symbolic vehicle for restoring the patient to a state of 'beauty'.

Shadow A powerful aspect of yourself – either positive or negative – that you may have trouble acknowledging.

Siddhi An unusual skill or supernatural power acquired through meditation and spiritual practice.

Triple Goddess Maiden, mother and crone, as a representative of the cycles of life.

Wave–particle duality A central concept of quantum mechanics, which arose to address the inability of classical concepts to fully describe the behaviour of quantum-scale objects.

Wheel of Life mandala A teaching mandala whose purpose is to illustrate the essence of all the Buddha's teachings, which is contained in his Four Noble Truths.

Yantra A Hindu form of the mandala – a potent sacred symbol, a power diagram and a meditative tool for attaining realization of the One.

Index

Page numbers in *italics* refer to
illustration captions.

Acknowledgements

akg-images 204; Archives CDA/Guillot 207; R u S Michaud 167; The British Library 177

Alamy A Room with Views 147; Amana Images 243; Anthony Ling 187; The Art Gallery Collection 46; Beyond Fotomedia GmbH 97; Bruce McGowan 168; Chad Riley/UpperCut Images 175; Christopher Scott 269; Chuck Place 238; Corbis Super RF 290; Cultura RM 95; Gianni Dagli Orti/Art Archive 266; Godong/Robert Harding World Imagery 63; i love images 117; Imagestopshop 281; Inspirestock 159; JoeFoxDublin 61; Klaus Lang 22; Mary Evans Picture Library 50, 66; Mira 82; Pep Roig 18, 301; The Print Collector 31, 190; Rob Walls 172; Tim Gainey 6, 257; Trigger Image 303; View Stock 192

Bridgeman Art Library Dinodia 254; The Stapleton Collection 222

Corbis Alex Mares-Manton/Mind Body Soul 141; Alinari Archives 215; Bettmann 29; Burstein Collection 68; Charles and Josette Lenars 47, 235; Charles Krebs 289; Dan Brownsword/Cultura 103; Danilo Calilung 25; David Muench 34; Gavin Hellier/JAI 49; Godong/Robert Harding World Imagery 13; Image Source 98; Inspirestock 55; IPS/Monsoon/Photolibrary 39; JGI/Jamie Grill/Blend Images 127; Kate Kunz 149; Keren Su 261; Lindsay Hebberd 180; Lou Cypher 186; LWA/Stephen Welstead 107; Micha Pawlitzki 87; Mike Kepka/San Francisco Chronicle 161; Mirko Iannace 65; Moodboard 113; NASA 26; Ocean 121; Pierre Jacques/Hemis 78; Rudy Sulgan 91; The Stapleton Collection 223; Sylvain Sonnet 51; Tammy Hanratty 123; Tetra Images 145; Trinette Reed/Blend Images 220

Fotolia ABG 200; Alexa Catalin 119; AVAVA 137; Awe Inspiring Images 273; chiyacat 80–1; dean 153; East West Imaging 155; Elenathewise 72; Giorgio Clementi 278; Len Green 16; Marilyn Barbone 276; Martin Valigursky 274; Monkey Business 139; MyTrainArt 59; Pierre Graffan 292; Pippa West 42; Scrumsrus 227; Shariff Che'Lah 265; Stephane Benito 69; Stephane Pissavin 30; sveng 84; tiI5 248; WavebreakMediaMicro 157; Yuri Arcurs 143, 189

Getty Images AFP 244; Alistair Berg 194; Andrea Booher 74; Betsie Van Der Meer 129; Bridgeman Art Library 255 /Gottfried Lindauer 45; Danita Delimont 88; David Silverman 262; Godong/Robert Harding

World Imagery 179, 184, 253; Jamie Grill 131; Jean Michel Foujols 101; Jean-Yves Bruel 33; John Slater 105; Jose Luis Pelaez 115; Kathy Collins 218; Lanz von Horsten/Gallo Images 135; Sarah-Jane Joel 236; SuperStock 201; Thomas Barwick 2, 133; Tom Merton 111, 188

Giulia Hetherington 211

Mary Evans Picture Library Interfoto/Bildarchiv Hansmann 164

MWM Graphics Matt W Moore 287

NASA NASA/ESA/Hubble Heritage (STScI/AURA)-ESA/Hubble Collaboration 12

Octopus Publishing Group 271, 272 above, 277, 295; Paul Bricknell 11; Russell Sadur 99, 173; Ruth Jekinson 56, 299, 305; William Reavell 94

Photolibrary Group Amana Images 53; artparadigm 199; The British Library 9; Daniel Dancer/Still Pictures 247; Fancy Collection 151; Luca Tettoni/Robert Harding Travel 171; P Deliss/Godong 77; Paula Brinkman 283; Raphael Senzamici 251; Rieger-Renault 193; Roger Holden 163; Sue Bishop/Flowerphotos 20; Tao Images Ltd 197

Science Photo Library Christian Darkin 19; David Nunuk 41; Eckhard Slawk 36; Pasieka 15

Sonia Halliday Photographs 203, 208, 212

SuperStock Bridgeman Art Library 216; Cultura Ltd 109, 297; Eye Ubiquitous 228; Fancy Collection 125 above and below; imagebroker.net 285; Peter Willi 231

Susan St Thomas 241

TopFoto Charles Walker 258

Werner Forman Archive Fitzwilliam Museum, Cambridge 71

Senior Editor **Leanne Bryan**
Deputy Art Director **Yasia Williams-Leedham**
Designer **Tracy Killick Art Direction and Design**
Picture Researchers **Roland and Sarah Smithies**
Senior Production Controller **Lucy Carter**